SOCIOLOGY
AND
DEVELOPMENT

TONY BARNETT

HUTCHINSON

London   Melbourne   Sydney   Auckland   Johannesburg

Hutchinson Education

An imprint of Century Hutchinson Ltd
62–65 Chandos Place, London WC2N 4NW

Century Hutchinson Australia Pty Ltd
PO Box 496, 16–22 Church Street, Hawthorn,
Victoria 3122, Australia

Century Hutchinson New Zealand Limited
PO Box 40–086, Glenfield, Auckland 10,
New Zealand

Century Hutchinson South Africa (Pty) Ltd
PO Box 337, Bergvlei, 2012 South Africa

First published 1988

Set in Linotron Ehrhardt

Printed and bound in Great Britain by
Anchor Brendon Ltd, Tiptree, Essex

British Library Cataloguing in Publication Data

Barnett, Tony, *1945–*
  Sociology and development.
  1. Economic development—Social aspects
  2. Developing countries—Economic
  conditions
  I. Title
  306'.3'091724   HC59.7

ISBN 0 09 173002 3

Contents

Preface

This book is about sociology and development. It is neither a general account of development nor an attempt to explore questions of social policy in the Third World. Were it either of these, it would have been a very different book. I have concentrated on sociology rather than on policy or development because I believe that sociology, together with its related discipline, anthropology, provides valuable insights into the problems of development both in the 'Third World' (with which this book is mainly concerned) and in the so-called 'developed countries', and that a sociological perspective is a valuable tool.

I have been interested and involved in development in one way or another since 1962, beginning from a perspective which in 1963 led me to go as a volunteer teacher to Sierra Leone. At that time, I thought that development was a fairly straightforward problem, of education combined with charity. I returned after a year having learned that this was not the case; that the process (if it was a process) was infinitely more complicated, and required an understanding of the historical, cultural and political ways in which people organised their social lives.

For the last fourteen years, I have worked in the School of Development Studies at the University of East Anglia, Norwich. Our teaching here attempts an interdisciplinary approach to development, combining environmental sciences such as agronomy and soil science with social science insights. I have learned from my colleagues and from my students some of the ways in which these different disciplines can contribute to a fuller understanding. Also during these years, I have had a number of opportunities to work at the 'sharp end' of development – in a planning office in Papua New Guinea, in a cooperative ministry in Jordan, and on a rural development project in Zambia among others. In all of these places I have learned much.

Among the lessons I have learned is the value of a sociological perspective, something which I once doubted. Today,
the main problems in the Third World are not, by and large,
the absence of technical specialists – countries such as India
and Pakistan have these aplenty; countries which lack such
expertise can often purchase it. The main problems are sociological and political problems, the contexts within which apparently 'technical' decisions are taken. One example of this which
is commonly used (and which I use in this book) is that of the
Green Revolution – a package of 'technical' changes aimed at
increasing agricultural production. The lesson we have learned
from that experiment (an experiment which has touched the
lives of millions of people) is that efficient production does not
lead directly, or at all, to social justice. Indeed, in some cases,
it may lead to increased poverty and misery.

Inevitably, such conclusions mean that much in this book
has a political complexion. This is to be expected, given that
any discussion of human social relations is bound to concern
itself with relative power and control over the various resources
on which power is founded. Because social power takes many
forms – economic, cultural, sexual – I believe that an understanding of the relation between sociology and the analysis
of development can tell us a great deal about how and why
development had occurred and how and why it might or might
not occur. As I emphasise throughout the book, I also believe
that such a study tells us as much about the developed world
as it does about the underdeveloped world. I have tried to avoid
setting up a gross dichotomy between those of us who live in
the 'developed' countries and those who live in the 'underdeveloped' countries. There are differences between the societies of
these two worlds, otherwise such a book would hardly be
necessary. But we are all citizens of the same world, and the
history of that world during the past five hundred years has
made us all more interdependent. Increasingly, we share
resources, ideas and experiences which are common, but we
share them unequally. Sociology can tell us a great deal about
the origins of this inequality and how it is maintained.

I have tried very hard to make the book easily readable so

that it can be as useful to the first-year sociology student as to the more advanced. To this end, I have employed boxes throughout the text, and these are intended to do two types of thing. In some cases, they provide examples and illustrations of general theoretical points; in others, they elaborate on the more difficult ideas. The intention is that the reader should choose when to read straight through the text and when to look in the boxes for help or for additional information. I recognise that some of the terms are difficult. For that reason, I have provided a glossary at the end of the book, and indicated which words are to be found in the glossary by printing them in bold on their first appearance.

Many people have helped me in writing this book. Murray Morrison and Mary Maynard read and commented in detail on earlier drafts. Frank Ellis read some chapters. Many of my students read all or part of it and I have incorporated a lot of their criticisms. Sarah Knights, as well as being a very dear and special friend, proof-read and commented on a number of drafts as well as putting up with bouts of bad-temper. My children, Jacob and Helen, tolerated considerable absence of mind on my part as well as absence overseas, and also discussed many of the issues with me at one time or another, even if they didn't know it at the time! Maureen Grimsley provided practical support by preventing the house from becoming chaotic.

Perhaps my greatest debt, however, is to the many people of the Third World with whom I have lived or worked at one time or another. To list them by name would be difficult, but in particular, the pupils at the Methodist Secondary School, Kailahun, Sierra Leone (1963–4), the people of Nueila village in the Sudan, the staff of the Central (now National) Planning Office, Papua New Guinea, and various cadres of the Eritrean People's Liberation Front, have all been my teachers.

Tony Barnett
Norwich 1987

Part One

INTRODUCTION
AND
OVERVIEW

1

Feeling the effects of development

The Labour Migrant

Imagine that you have been unable to find a job in your home town. Your family can no longer help you with money, the situation at home has become intolerable. You pack your more precious and necessary possessions and take off for another town, or even another country, aiming to make a new start. When you arrive at your destination, you are confronted by a large number of problems which need urgent solutions. You need food and shelter most urgently, but soon you will also need friends. You may speak with a different accent from the people in your new place, or you may even speak a different language. You have become a labour migrant.

Now imagine that you live in the African Sahel, that broad belt of desert and semi-desert which stretches across the northern half of the continent. There has been a drought which has gone on for years. The grazing has disappeared and as a result your family's cattle are dead. For the past four years, the sparse crops which used to be grown have failed. There is no food locally, and the government has been unable to provide any relief. Indeed it has refused to admit that there is a problem, fearing that doing so might make the international banks, to which it is indebted, lose confidence, and reluctant to lend it any more money.

You decide to travel to the capital city, some 500 km away. After a difficult journey, mostly on foot, occasionally hitch-hiking, you arrive and are faced with the problems of food, shelter, work, friends. Once again you are a labour migrant.

It is quite possible that in the first case, you couldn't find a job because of the decline of some industry which had provided employment for your parents and grandparents. The industrial decline may have been the result of the loss of markets, because there were no longer colonies which had the habit of buying the products made in your town, or because other countries were able to produce those things more cheaply. In the second case, the effects of the drought may have been felt particularly keenly because your family's traditional grazing land had been lost – perhaps an overseas company had leased part of it from the government, the part which was only used at times of very severe drought.

What is common to both of these situations is that you have been forced to make decisions, confront problems, not because you chose to, but because of events beyond your control.

Making Sense of the World

How can the sociology of development help us to make sense of this kind of situation? In many ways, sociology is always trying to make sense of the 'outsideness', the 'otherness' which we all feel when we find that we cannot do what we as individuals want because there are rules (legal – written down and administered by courts; moral – beliefs about what are 'self evidently' right ways to behave; religious – supported by beliefs in non-human agency) which prevent us.

Sociology was described by one of its early researchers, Emile Durkheim, as being the study of 'social facts' (see box 1.1).

Box 1.1 *Social facts*

'. . . that group of phenomena which may be differentiated from those studied by the other natural sciences. When I fulfil my obligations as brother, husband or citizen, when I execute my contracts, I perform duties which are defined, externally to myself and my acts, in laws and in custom. Even if they conform to my own sentiments and I feel their reality subjectively, such reality is still objective, for I did not create them; I merely

---

inherited them through my education. . . . Here, then, is a category of facts with very distinctive characteristics: it consists of ways of acting, thinking and feeling, external to the individual, and endowed with a power of coercion, by reason of which they control him.'

(Durkheim, E., *The Rules of Sociological Method*, The Free Press, New York, 1964 pp. 1–3, first published in French in 1893, in English, 1933.)

What Durkheim was trying to pin down was the study of the otherness of society as it constrains or limits individual wishes and ambitions. He was asking how human societies ensure some degree of order, of regularity, of agreed rules of behaviour. In particular, he was concerned to discover how a moral community could be established during a time of great social, economic and cultural change.

This chapter was deliberately introduced with the image of the labour migrant. This is because throughout history, removed from their familiar surroundings and way of life, such people have always had to find ways of making a new life with new rules. Labour migrants have had to find new ways of solving the problems of order and morality as a result of the disruption resulting from changes affecting their lives. Such changes have included the slave trade (a vicious and enforced form of labour migration), the Scottish Highland clearances of the eighteenth century (see box 1.2), the movement of people from southern Europe to be 'guestworkers' in Germany, or more recently, skilled workers going from unemployment in the UK to high wages in the Gulf.

Box 1.2 *The Highland clearances*

From about 1775 onwards, the already impoverished small farmers of the Scottish Highlands were increasingly displaced as their land was taken over for profitable sheep-grazing. The English and Lowland Scot landlords raised rents, and a massive migration to North America began – for example to Nova

Scotia (New Scotland) in Canada. Somebody writing in 1807 described one of these migrations:

'The inhabitants of one district were required to pay an augmented rent for their ... (land) ... on which ... they barely kept body and soul together.... They therefore took the unanimous resolution of seeking a new habitation in the wildest region of America ... they hired vessels to transport 500 people to Canada; and the whole district took their departure – men with their pregnant wives, their children running at their feet and clinging to the breast – all, all took their departure, casting many a longing look at their well known and favourite mountains.'

(Richards, E., *A History of the Highland Clearances*, Croom Helm, 1983, p. 203.)

I have used the image of the labour migrant because, as well as making links from the past to the present, it also makes a link to a particular part of the past, the late eighteenth and early nineteenth centuries, when there was considerable population movement within European countries. This was the result of radical changes in the organisation of both agricultural and industrial production. It was this period of radical change, as capitalism spread to become the dominant economic system, which gave rise to labour migration from one rural area to another, from country to town, and to the growth of cities (see box 1.3). It also led to the development of 'sociology' as an area of study – an attempt to understand the confusion, a science which could bring about order in this suddenly changing and confusing world.

Box 1.3 *The creation of labourers in England*

Writing in 1795, an observer of the English rural scene noted the following:

'The practice of enlarging and engrossing (*joining together*) of farms, especially that of depriving the peasantry of all landed property, have contributed greatly to increase the number of dependent poor.

The landowner, to render his income adequate to the increased expense of living, unites several small farms into one, raises the rent to the utmost, and avoids the expense of repairs. The rich farmer also engrosses as many farms as he is able to stock; lives in more credit and comfort than he could otherwise do; and out of the profits of the several farms, makes an ample provision for one family. Thus the thousands of families, which formerly gained an independent livelihood on those separate farms, have been gradually reduced to the class of day-labourers. But day-labourers are sometimes in want of work, and are sometimes unable to work; and in either case their resort is to the parish. . . . And in the proportion as the number of farming families has decreased, the number of poor families has increased.'

(Rev. Davies, D., The Case of the Labourers in Husbandry, 1795, quoted in Cole, G. D. H. and Filson, A. W., *The British Working Class Movements: Selected Documents 1789–1875*, St. Martin's Press, New York, 1967, p. 3.)

This extract illustrates the effects of both the so-called industrial and agricultural revolutions. New technology meant that less labour was required for agricultural production and more for industry. Thus there was surplus of rural labour, and a process of stepped migration occurred. Labourers near the new factories moved to work in them; their places were taken by others from further away. In this way labour was redistributed across the whole country. But the process took time, and often there were pockets of surplus labour. These people had to be supported by the local parish.

A similar process of 'labour transfer' from rural to urban areas is taking place in many countries in Africa, Asia and Latin America today.

Sociology has its roots in the attempt to understand change.

Thus it is that the sociology of development encompasses all sociology. The question of what 'development' means will appear and reappear throughout this book, along with another one – why should we choose to use a word like 'development' (implying getting better – in other words a *value* laden word) when the other word 'change' might seem quite adequate? Box 1.4 explores some of the meanings of the word 'development'. We shall look in more detail at some of the problems of defining development in chapter 9.

Box 1.4 *What do we mean by development?*

In trying to answer this question I will talk in terms of three meanings and three problem areas.

The three meanings:
Development from within: this view says that any object – a plant, an animal, a society – has within it the tendency to change its form. When we talk about societies in this way, we assume that the possibilities and the direction of change are the result only of processes within that society.

Development as interaction: this view says that development of anything results from the interaction of an object and its environment. Thus, an animal or a society changes because of a combination of the qualities and potentials within the object and the opportunities and resources available in the environment.

Development as interpenetration: this view says that we cannot really draw a sharp distinction between an object and its environment. For example, an animal is made of materials from outside itself; its actions in feeding and housing itself alter that environment. When applied to society, this view raises the question of where are the boundaries of any society? How can we distinguish sociologically between, for example, Egyptian society – which is predominantly Muslim – and its 'environment' which also contains many other Muslim countries, the

---

ideas, concerns and people of which may affect what goes on in Egypt.

Three problem areas:

Each of the meanings of development can be applied to any number of problems, depending upon what we decide to focus. For example, we could be concerned with the development of the family and look at it in any of the three ways that I have described. It is usual in the sociology of development to be concerned with development at one or all of the following three levels – social, cultural and political.

This approach provides us with a neat table which shows that the three problem areas can each be analysed in three ways. You might like to look at this table and think about the implications of each of the nine possible approaches.

	Development		
	from within	*interaction*	*interpenetration*
Social	1	2	3
Cultural	4	5	6
Political	7	8	9

Max Weber tried to understand some of the causes and consequences of labour migration in Germany in the early and middle parts of the nineteenth century, when much 'development' was occurring in Europe (see box 1.5).

Box 1.5 *Weber on labour migration*

'Weber emphasised that the capitalist transformation of labour relations in eastern Germany had tended to depress the workers' standard of living ... and he pointed to the frequent employment of women, the barracks-like living quarters of day labourers and their families, and the lack of wage supplements in the form of ... gardening or a few head of cattle. This

---

proletarianisation* of rural labourers was aggravated because employers resorted to the employment of Polish and Russian migrants – a preference due only in part to the foreigners' willingness to work for lower wages, since their productivity also was lower than that of German workers. Polish and Russian workers were obedient because of their precarious status. They were also strictly seasonal labourers who could be forced back across the frontier, relieving their employers of the burden of any financial or administrative obligations.

The German workers were more demanding than the migrants in regard to nutrition and conditions of work, and because of these higher demands they lost out in the competition with Poles and Russians.'

(Bendix, R., *Max Weber: an intellectual portrait*, Methuen, 1962, pp. 19–20.)

Sociology as Biography and History

Sociology has been described as at least in part concerned with the intersection of *biography* and *history*. This is an important idea, because it directs our attention to two aspects of our study. One is the relatedness of different 'disciplines' which might appear to be quite separate. In fact, disciplines like sociology, anthropology, economics, economic history, history, geography, are only separate because people choose to make them so. As you read on, you will discover that this separation can be a hindrance to thought, it can make us think we have seen a problem in all its aspects when in fact we have excluded many relevant ideas and much information which might help us to understand the problem we are looking at. For example, if we were concerned with the question 'what causes labour migration from a particular region?' we would be giving a very partial answer if we only looked at the immediate causes, such as unemployment. A more satisfactory answer to the question

*Words in bold in the text are explained in the Glossary, page 219.

would require that we examine the economic history of the particular region in order to understand why there was unemployment, and whether or not it was likely to be long-term or short-term.

The Sociology of Development

This discussion may seem to have come a long way from the sociology of development. But we are looking at just the kinds of questions with which all sociology is concerned, and which the sociology of development approaches in particular ways. It asks how social change occurs, what we mean by social change, how it affects individuals, how it affects whole societies, and most recently, how it affects the whole world taken as one 'social system'.

Sociology, Development and Evolution

There are some parallels between labour migration in contemporary Africa and in nineteenth century Europe. This is not to say that they both have the same causes or effects. Rather it suggests that some of the human experiences of that process might be similar. I mentioned earlier that it was in the very radical social changes which became evident in Europe in the early nineteenth century that we can discover the roots of sociology and of the sociology of development. In some respects, many of the ideas, theories, prejudices and opinions which informed nineteenth century thinkers still influence the way that we think about social and economic problems.

For example, some people talk about the '**evolution**' of society in the Third World. 'Evolution' was a favourite word in the nineteenth century, and the recently formulated 'theory' of evolution was said to explain many things, from political life through to the development of the family. But think also about the use of the terms 'modern' and 'traditional' when they are applied to social organisation and ways of behaving in society. Isn't that a disguised use of the idea of 'evolution'? In fact,

Western social thought and Western life, despite its concern with the 'new' and the 'modern', is still very much influenced by the ideas of the nineteenth century. This should not surprise us very greatly because the world as we have come to know it, with its rapid communications, large scale units of political organisation, international trade, international banking, rapid technological change, has only been created in the past 150 years, and we are still trying to make sense of it. That is why it is always necessary in looking at the sociology of development to have at the back of our minds a fairly clear idea of what the early sociologists had to say. It will also be useful to have an idea of what the word 'theory' means, because we are, after all, talking about *social theory*.

An important point to notice about any theory is that it sets out the agenda for discussion and research. It says what is relevant and what is not. So, the ways in which questions are asked often depend on the theories that we begin with. Box 1.4 showed that there are different meanings and levels in the way that we use the word development. Each of these is a different theory. In box 1.6 we look a little more closely at what we mean by the word theory.

Box 1.6 *Theory*

'Theory', both in everyday conversation and in its more precise form, in science, always poses questions in particular ways, defines the meanings of words in specific ways, includes some possibilities and excludes others. A 'theory' is never 'true' – rather it should be seen as being a very special form of language which sketches out the words we can use to discuss a particular problem and the ways in which we can test our language description against our experience. In the same way that it would be faintly absurd to ask whether the English, Russian or Swahili languages are 'true', so it is not relevant to ask whether the specialised 'theory language' we use in sociology or any other area of study is 'true'. Rather, we should be asking whether it is *adequate* for the job it is being asked to do. The

---

English language is not very good at describing the life-world of, say, the !Kung* people of Southern Africa, because it was not invented to do that job. Similarly, the theoretical language of **functionalist sociology** has difficulty in describing and making sense of a society undergoing rapid change. In these senses, both English and functionalism are inadequate for those purposes. This problem becomes rather more complex (and interesting) in social science because social theory, being a produced thing – the result of people working/thinking together – reflects the experience and particular view of those who produce that theory. It often tends to support the beliefs which the theory producing group or groups hold about the way society is or ought to be working. It can therefore be said to *legitimate* their position, and thus, as the sociologist Karl Mannheim said, to become an **'ideology'** as well as a 'theory'. The switch from theory to ideology can occur in all sciences (remember Galileo), not only in sociology. There is a constant tendency to slide from what at first sight may appear to be a statement of 'fact' (something we know and agree to be 'true'), to a statement of 'value' (something about which we can disagree and about which we can never finally know the truth). If you want to read some more about this kind of problem, you should read G. Rose, *Deciphering Sociological Research*, Macmillan, London, 1979.

Evolutionary theory invites us to look at the world in a particular way, and to ask certain questions and not others. An example of an evolutionary approach might be a theory of political development which says that societies pass through a number of stages, starting with rule by one person who tells everyone else what they must do, and then moves through intermediate stages to a system in which there is some form of parliamentary democracy such as exists in western Europe.

It may be possible to perceive that kind of developmental sequence in history, but it is another thing to say that it *must* happen that way or that it *ought* to. To say the latter is to make

*See explanation in box 8.4, page 156.

a **value judgement**. And in fact, exactly that kind of judgement has been made, and is made, about the development of political arrangements in many parts of the world.

For example, in western Europe and North America, we tend to think that our system is democratic and 'best', and that this democracy is the end-product of a long process of evolution. However, in many parts of Africa, people believe that our system discriminates against the poor, and that a 'one party state' is more democratic, because it ensures that the poor are adequately represented.

The Early Sociologists

Having looked briefly at theory and at the nature of the sociology of development, we can now go on to look at the intellectual origins of the subject and its own development up to the present, bearing in mind that although the theory we began by discussing was created during another century, there is a surprising continuity both in the style of theory produced and in the problems that that theory is being required to explain.

The hundred years from 1750 to 1850 was a period of enormous change in western Europe – change in the ways people lived, and in the ways they thought, and, importantly for us, in the ways they thought about how they lived. All the criteria of right and wrong, moral and immoral, even of true and false, were changing as agricultural production changed and large scale manufacture developed, concentrated into towns and factories, using workers paid with money. The French historian, Fernand Braudel, expresses something of the flavour of these changes in the following quotation:

In the changing appearance of cities like London and Paris was reflected the transition from one way of life and art of living to another. The world of the *ancien regime*, very largely a rural one, was slowly but surely collapsing and being wiped out.

(Braudel, F., *The Structures of Everyday Life*, William Collins & Sons, 1981, p. 557.)

You should note two things about this quotation. One is that although Braudel talks about western Europe as the centre of the changes, they were changes which had already begun to affect, and were increasingly going to affect, the whole world. The other is Braudel's use of the slightly unusual term 'the art of living'. The unusualness may have caught your eye. What he is emphasising is that the very texture and feel, the 'structures of everyday life', had begun to change. In other words, not only was society changing, but the way it felt to be an individual was itself changing. When you visit a new place, perhaps another country or an unfamiliar part of your own country, you experience a hint of that strangeness. Imagine that feeling magnified several hundred times, and you will have some idea of how life must have felt for many people during this period.

Different groups in society will have experienced the strangeness and responded to it in different ways. Those most radically affected – the people driven from their land by the changes in agricultural production, the introduction of machinery, crop rotation, new, more concentrated land ownership – experienced something akin to our labour migrants. Their responses were variously to oppose the changes by rebellions of various kinds, or to form mutual aid societies in the towns: in other words to create a new world, a new 'art of living'. Those who in some respects were least immediately affected, insofar as they did not have to struggle to live, responded by thinking about the changes, trying to make intellectual rather than practical sense of them. They produced theories.

August Comte

In particular, the French aristocrat Saint-Simon (1760–1825) and his follower and pupil Auguste Comte (1798–1857), can be seen as original sociologists of development. This is particularly true of the latter. Comte's theory expresses very clearly two sets of ideas which were very influential in his time, and which (in different forms) remain so in our own. These are the idea of evolutionary change and the related idea of progressive change through the development of the human intellect, and in particular through its development in scientific thought (see box 1.7).

Box 1.7 *Comte and the reorganisation of society*

Impressed by the progress of science, Comte believed it could provide the way forward to a harmonious society based on a science of politics and social administration. He wrote:

'Before the introduction of the Positive Sciences into Europe all special as well as general knowledge was either theological or metaphysical ... the natural sciences, more and more, sought for a basis in observation and experiment ... the sciences successively became more positive ... as they were more or less closely related to man. Thus astronomy first, then physics, later chemistry and finally, in our own day physiology, have been constituted as positive sciences. ... The influence of theology and metaphysics on these subjects has already been destroyed in the eyes of all educated men. ... The realisation of this condition is alone wanting for the spiritual development of the new social system. ...'

(Comte, A., *A Brief Appraisal of Modern History*)

'In the last resort all resolves itself into establishing ... a positive theory in politics distinct from practice, and one which shall bring our social system into harmony with the present state of knowledge. Pursuing this course of reflection we shall perceive that the above conclusions may be resumed in a single conception: scientific men ought in our day to elevate politics to the ranks of a science of observation.'

(Comte, A., *Plan for Reorganising Society*)

(Both of these extracts are in Fletcher, R., *The Crisis of Industrial Civilisation*, Heinemann Educational books, 1974, pages 9 and 134 respectively.)

Comte believed that the human mind, human society and human knowledge all went through a process of development and change, from non-scientific, authoritarian, and what he called 'metaphysical' (meaning based on belief, faith, non-human agency) to a state of rational scientific knowledge – which he called 'positivism' – which could be applied to the solution of social problems. So, the idea of scientific control, or at least guidance, of social life appears very early on in the development of sociology. Indeed, Comte considered that sociology would be the 'Queen of the sciences', providing the 'truth' about how to organise society so that it would be free of the conflict and confusion which was so evident then, and which continues in our own time (see box 1.8).

Box 1.8 *Problems and puzzles*

It is worth giving a little thought to the idea that social *problems* can be 'solved', as though they are like crossword *puzzles* with one correct solution. It is easy to confuse the meanings of two words which are in fact very different although we sometimes use them interchangeably. It may be more useful to say that puzzles are things which have correct or incorrect solutions, whereas problems do not, by and large, have solutions, but rather 'resolutions', settlements, outcomes which are 'satisfactory' rather than 'correct' or 'true'. Most of the things that we are concerned with in social science are problems and not puzzles for the simple reason that human beings always see things from different points of view, even define problems differently, and have to come to arrangements which are more or less satisfactory. Note here that Durkheim's view that sociology should study social phenomena 'objectively as external things', may have been useful from the point of view of suggesting greater rigour in the research methods to be used; it could never have been a useful suggestion as to the way in which we can finally know the social world. 'Social facts' may be thought about as though they are things; but their actual 'thingness' can never be finally known and defined, for social

---

experience is always lived through human consciousness, and each consciousness is the outcome of the peculiar interaction of biography and history which we have already noted. Treating social problems as though they are puzzles is to act as though the 'thingness' of the social world is uncontentious. It is also to fall into the trap of **'utopianism'** – a view of social reality which says that perfection of some kind, usually perfect harmony, can be achieved.

In many respects, Comte's view of sociology contained the illusion that through the application of better developed science, social harmony could be achieved.

Utopiansim

This tendency to utopian thinking, the idea that a perfect, conflict-free social world might be created, has often appeared in sociological theories of change and development. Karl Marx (and Friedrich Engels), in an attempt to combat this tendency in the social and political thought of their time, wrote an essay called 'Socialism – Scientific and Utopian'. This tried to show the differences between a social science which analyses the world objectively and a social science which starts from a view of how the world ought to be, and then tries to show how this can be achieved. It is, though, a difficult problem to escape from, because a hundred years later, Dahrendorf was attacking the same problem in another form in his essay 'Out of Utopia' which criticised functionalism in the following terms:

All utopias from Plato's Republic to George Orwell's brave new world of 1984 have one element in common: they are all societies from which change is absent. Whether conceived as a final state and climax of historical development, as an intellectual's nightmare, or as a romantic dream, the social fabric of utopias does not, and perhaps cannot, recognise the unending flow of the historical process.

(Dahrendorf, R., Out of Utopia, in his *Essays in the Theory of Society*, Routledge and Kegan Paul, 1968, p. 105.)

In view of this continuing concern with utopias which appears (albeit in different forms) in both the early sociologists such as Comte and in functionalism such as that of Talcott Parsons, it is useful to understand something of how sociological theory itself developed in the nineteenth and early twentieth centuries.

Spencer, Tonnies and Durkheim

During the nineteenth and early twentieth centuries, many theorists attempted to make sense of the changes going on around them. The problem that intrigued them was the way in which society seemed to have become more 'complex', with greater specialisation both in terms of what individuals did, and in what different parts of society did. Thus we find Herbert Spencer (1820–1903) not only comparing society to a biological organism, but insisting that 'Society is an Organism' – which is the title of chapter two of his book *The Evolution of Society* (see box 1.9). Spencer understood the term 'development' in the sense of development from within.

Box 1.9 *Spencer, development and differentiation*

Spencer considered that societies and biological organisms followed the same laws of development. He said:

'It is . . . a character of social bodies, as of living bodies, that while they increase in size they increase in structure. Like low animals, the embryo of a high one has few distinguishable parts, but while it is acquiring greater mass, its parts multiply and differentiate. It is thus with society. At first the unlikeness among its groups of units are inconspicuous in number and degree, but as population augments, divisions and subdivisions become more numerous and more decided. Further, in the social organism as in the individual organism, differentiation ceases only with that completion of the type which marks maturity and precedes decay . . . the lowest type of animal is

---

all stomach, all respiratory surface, all limbs. . . . Similarly in a society. . . . While rudimentary, a society is all warrior, all hunter, all hut-builder, all tool-maker: every part fulfils for itself all needs . . . a social organism and an individual organism are entirely alike. When we see that in a mammal arresting the lungs quickly brings the heart to a stand, that if the stomach fails absolutely . . . all other parts . . . cease to act . . . mutual dependence of parts is an essential characteristic. And when, in a society, we see that the workers in iron stop if the miners do not supply materials, that makers of clothes cannot carry on their business in the absence of those who spin and weave textile fabrics . . . we are obliged to say that this mutual dependence of parts is similarly rigorous.'

(Spencer, E., *The Evolution of Society*, University of Chicago Press, Chicago and London, 1967, pp. 3–5.)

Adopting a similar view of development as development from within, Ferdinand Tonnies (1855–1936) was mainly concerned with the changes in the moral and ethical bases of society and the quality of the relationships between its members. He wrote of a transition, gradual and uneven, which he summarised in terms of two polar types. He called these polar types, which are not unlike Max Weber's 'ideal types', **Gemeinschaft** and **Gesellschaft**. These words cannot be directly translated into English but are usually taken to mean respectively 'community' and 'association'.

This division into two opposite types draws attention to the idea that in the past, and in some parts of Europe and other places beyond Europe, society had been, and was still, organised in terms of very close, direct interpersonal knowledge and shared beliefs. Everybody knew what was going on, saw their neighbours frequently, exchanged ideas, came to decisions, had disagreements. Even if people did not know each other, they shared broadly the same values and attitudes. By contrast, associational society was more complex, with many intermediaries between the individual and the society to which s/he belonged. This complexity of relationships allowed for the growth of individual differences.

Emile Durkheim (1858–1917) dealt with the same problem in a similar way, and talked about two types of **social solidarity**. By 'solidarity', Durkheim meant the moral beliefs and ideas which formed the 'commonsense' underlying social life. Mechanical solidarity (characteristic of pre-industrial societies) was said to be based on agreement and identity between people; organic solidarity derived from agreement to tolerate a range of differences, conflicts being moderated through a variety of institutional arrangements, such as courts, trades unions and political parties. In pre-industrial societies there is little or no division of labour, everyone works in similar ways and consumes in similar ways: equally there is little division of opinion, little individuality. Indeed, Durkheim says that 'the more primitive societies are, the more resemblances there are among individuals' (Durkheim, E., 1965, p. 133). He carried this view to an extreme when he wrote that 'among barbarous peoples there is found a physiognomy [type of face] peculiar to the horde rather than individual physiognomies' (Durkheim, E., 1964, p. 133).

We can look at some of the wider implications of this view; but first let us try to understand what the other type of society was supposed to be like.

Society Based on Organic Solidarity

Durkheim saw this as the opposite of the first type. Organic solidarity is characteristic of societies which have an advanced division of labour, where production, distribution and consumption are carried out in many and specialised ways. Individuals do not do the same or even similar work – it is the kind of society with which most of us are familiar. It is a society in which there is considerable difference of opinion on all kinds of subjects – with just the kind of potentially confusing mental world that I said earlier seemed to have developed in Europe and North America during the nineteenth century. It was the contrast between this world and another that Durkheim and the others were trying to produce a theoretical language to describe (see box 1.10). But the way in which they posed the problem, and the assumptions that they started with, determined – at least in part – the answer (see box 1.6). This is most evident in the two very short quotations from Durkheim which you have just read where he is writing as a social evolutionist.

Box 1.10 *Durkheim's language*

You will recall that he used the term 'primitive' and that he subscribed to the view that in 'primitive' societies, people bear a very close physical resemblance to each other. These two views raise the following problems.

Durkheim knew nothing at first hand about other, non-European societies. Of course, this was impossible as far as historical societies were concerned. But in principle he could have gained firsthand knowledge of the non-European societies of his time; he could, for example have travelled to Australia to study the native Australian peoples whom he used extensively in support of his arguments. In fact, much of his information about these people came from the very unscientifically assembled accounts of 'travellers'. Secondly, he assumed that these people could be safely described as 'primitive' – remember the subtle relationship between the theory producers and their own place in their biographical/historical time, and then remember that Durkheim was writing at the time when both France and Britain had assembled and were now administering great colonial empires. Thirdly, and related to the easy use of the term 'primitive', you should be aware of the evolutionary core to Durkheim's work, his belief in 'progress'. Thus, for Durkheim, and many other thinkers of the nineteenth and early twentieth centuries, sociology, insofar as it was to be about change, was also without question about an historical journey of 'progress' which terminated in western Europe. In other words, they saw their world and its political organisation into empires as evidence of a process of 'social evolution'.

Nineteenth century Europeans were very enthusiastic about organising 'Great Exhibitions' of one kind or another to show off their progress. The Crystal Palace in London was built for just such an exhibition. These exhibitions often had sections which represented 'progress' as it was supposed to affect the peoples of the colonial Empires. The aim was to lay out for the visitor evidence of the differences in the levels of civilisation of disparate forms of human society.

To do justice to Durkheim, like his near contemporary Max Weber, he had a strong sense of the human costs of progress – social disruption and individual confusion – but this awareness was restricted to the impact of these things on his own society. They were not seen as problems for the 'primitive' societies of the colonies.

Evolutionism plus Functionalism

As well as writing as an evolutionist, Durkheim was also a key thinker in the development of functionalist explanation in sociology. Like Spencer he considered that society could be thought about as though it were an organism. This kind of social theory is called functionalism, and is summed up in the following quotation:

The word function is used in two quite different senses. Some-times it suggests a system of vital movements, without reference to their consequences; at others it expresses the relation existing between these movements and corresponding needs of the organism. Thus, we speak of the function of digestion, respir-ation &c; but we also say that digestion has as its function the incorporation into the organism of liquid or solid substances designed to replenish its losses, that respiration has for its function the introduction of necessary gases into the tissues of an animal for the sustainment of life &c. It is in the second sense that we shall use the term. To ask what the function of the division of labour is, is to seek for the need which it supplies.

(Durkheim, E., 1965, p. 49.)

From a functionalist point of view, the institutions of society, such as those of political life or the family or the economy, are to be explained in terms of the contributions they make to its overall health and welfare. It follows from his perspective that a society can be 'healthy' or 'ill', 'normal' or 'abnormal'. Where moral values are unclear, society is in an unhealthy, 'anomic' state. In Durkheim's words: 'the cause . . . of the incessantly recurrent conflicts, and the multifarious disorders of which the economic world exhibits so sad a spectacle', and which is an 'unhealthy phenomenon' which 'runs counter to the aim of society, which is to supress, or at least to moderate, war among men. . . .' (Durkheim, E., 1965, pp. 2–3).

We can see from this that the 'healthy' society – the 'normal' society – for Durkheim is a society which is harmonious. In this type of theory, conflict is destructive, not creative. This, as we shall see, is a view with which the Marxist tradition in sociology would very strongly disagree. What Durkheim provides then, if we use him as a kind of summary of sociological theory in the nineteenth and early twentieth centuries, is a potent mixture:

EVOLUTIONISM plus FUNCTIONALISM.

I have given so much attention to Durkheim because his theories exercised a very powerful influence over both the sociology of development and the related discipline of social anthropology. Until about the middle of the 1960s most sociologists and social anthropologists (and even a lot of economists) who thought about development and change asked their questions in ways similar to Durkheim. This was not only because of his influence but also because these kinds of ideas were very generally accepted at that time. Remember what was said earlier about theory being a 'satisfactory' language for describing experience, and also a legitimation of an existing state of affairs. The kinds of idea which were current, and which Durkheim reflected, were convenient for those who had deep-seated beliefs in the values of Western society and in progress towards that type of society (see box 1.11).

Box 1.11 *Durkheim and science*

Durkheim's writing was also concerned with the method of social research and social theory, and he endeavoured to make it 'scientific' so that it could provide a guide to action, to the way that social life should be lived in order to create happiness – which he identified with social harmony. In this respect, he was continuing the tradition of Comte; he was also setting a precedent for later sociologists – trying to provide a scientific expertise which would form the basis for the action of the informed policy maker and sincere politician. He said 'If (I) separate carefully the theoretical from the practical problems, it is not to the neglect of the latter, but, on the contrary, to be in a better position to solve them.'

(Durkheim, E., 1965, p. 33)

This tradition of thought continued and continues today. For example, the title which the United Nations Development Programme gives to those it employs is 'expert'. These 'experts', some of whom are sociologists and social anthropologists, are in some way supposed to provide 'objective' scientific knowledge with the aim of bringing about 'development'.

Such attempts to apply scientific method to the study of society are sometimes called '**positivism**'.

Modernisation Theory

Later work in the sociology and social anthropology of development, by many different writers (Redfield, 1953; Parsons, 1966; Levy, 1966; Eisenstadt, 1963; Moore, 1963), followed in Durkheim's footsteps. For most of these writers, although the theoretical language changes and is less antiquated (if at times less elegant – see the extracts by Chodak (pp. 183–4) and by Eisenstadt (pp. 185–6) – the assumptions are broadly similar to those of Durkheim.

These thinkers are often described as *modernisation* theorists; their work contains the same potent elements as Durkheim's:

EVOLUTIONISM plus FUNCTIONALISM plus
POSITIVISM.

The following extract by Wilbert Moore, writing in 1963, is an example of this mixture. In it he describes modernisation as:

... a 'total' transformation of a traditional or pre-modern society into the types of technology and associated social organisation that characterises the 'advanced', economically prosperous and relatively politically stable nations of the Western World.

(Moore, W. E., *Social Change*, Prentice Hall, New Jersey, 1964, p. 89.)

There are features which are found in all modernisation theory, and which arise from the combination of evolutionism, functionalism and positivism. These features are:

1. Development takes place from within a society – external events such as colonialism and cultural influences are not particularly important.

2. Development follows essentially the same pattern in all societies.

3. The end result of development is prosperity and 'relative' political stability.

4. The scientific study of history and society will enable us to identify patterns from the past experience of some countries, such as the United States and Britain, and use this knowledge to bring about the same results in the developing or underdeveloped countries.

The American economic historian Rostow summed up this approach succinctly when he wrote about the 'five stages of economic growth': a movement by societies through the stages of traditional society, a preconditions for development stage, a take-off, a drive to maturity, and finally, an age of high mass consumption (Rostow, 1960).

The Weberian Influence

There is another tradition of sociological theory which fed into development theory. This originated from the work of Max Weber (1864–1924), a near contemporary of Durkheim.

In many ways, Weber was much more directly concerned with the question of development, for his central problem was the explanation of the origins of capitalism (see box 1.12).

Box 1.12 *Capitalism*

Capitalism can be defined as the economic and social system based on the private individual endeavour of those with capital to invest, who produce by employing others, sell the products on a market, and reinvest the profits from their sales in expanding their wealth and the scale of their activities.

The important social inventions characteristic of this type of society are the *commodity* – the idea that most things (land, labour, blood) can be sold; and the *market* – a place, shops, the stock exchange, factory employment offices – in which commodities can be exchanged for each other or for cash. Some of these ideas are discussed in more detail in chapter 5.

Weber's best-known work is '*The Protestant Ethic and the Spirit of Capitalism*' which was published in Germany in 1922, and in English in 1930. In this he argues that, at least in part, the development of capitalism can be explained by looking at the change in the way some sections of western European and American society began to think, to see their place in the world, during the sixteenth to eighteenth centuries. It is important to remember that this was not the only book he wrote, and that his study of capitalism was only part of a much wider study, an ambitious sociological, historical and economic 'mental experiment'.

In this experiment he looked at a set of societies – Ancient Palestine, India, China, western Europe – with the intention of teasing out from complex historical information those factors which resulted in societies with similar levels of technology developing in such different directions. In particular, he wanted to find out why capitalist industrialisation became a society-wide system in Europe and not in the other places. His answer was that religious beliefs had at least something, probably a great deal, to do with it. In particular, he pointed to the influence of the French theologian Jean Calvin (1509–1564). Calvin believed that there was nothing that human beings could do to affect their fate after death. God's wisdom was absolute, He decided what was to happen. This was a little disturbing for those who believed it, for whatever kind of life they led, their fate was predestined. The only way out of this gross psychological insecurity was to believe that success or failure during your life might just give a clue as to whether you would be going to heaven or to hell. In order to receive some such sign, Weber argued, Calvinists worked very hard in whatever job they had, saved their money, lived frugally.

You may wonder what connection there is between an obscure French theologian and the development of capitalist society. The answer that Weber provides is that the spread of such a belief system, together with the social behaviour which went with it, fitted in very well with the activities of capitalists, and therefore contributed to the spread of such behaviour throughout society – even among those who were not themselves Calvinists. Weber emphasises that capitalism is not about greed for gain; that exists in many societies. He says:

Unlimited greed for gain is not in the least identical with capitalism, and still less with its spirit. Capitalism may even be identical with the restraint, or at least a rational tempering, of this irrational impulse. But capitalism is identical with the pursuit of profit, and forever renewed profit, by means of continuous, rational, capitalistic enterprise. For it must be so:

in a wholly capitalistic order of society, an individual capitalistic enterprise which did not take advantage of its opportunities for profit-making would be doomed to extinction.

(Weber, M., *The Protestant Ethic and the Spirit of Capitalism*, Unwin, 1967, p. 17.)

Box 1.13 *Weber and values*

You should note two points in relation to Weber's theory. The first is that, unlike the social evolutionists, he did not see any *necessary* pattern or direction of development in history. The second is that he did not try to adopt a positivist scientific method similar to that used by the physical sciences. Rather, he said societies have to be explained in their own terms, not in terms of general theories of the kind that we have seen Durkheim producing. While we can use rigorous and clear research techniques – surveys, documents – the theory we produce can only be a precise *description* of the way any particular society works, and the way we give that description will be strongly affected by the reasons that we have for asking the question in the first place. So Weber did not believe that you could approach any problem in sociology except from your own value position. This is important because in the very political waters of the sociology of development, some writers try to give an impression of scientific neutrality.

Weber's influence on development sociology and development thinking is not as direct as that of Durkheim. It has also been a selective influence. While he gave a lot of attention to historical scholarship, those influenced by him have not on the whole done the same (see box 1.13). Instead, two parts of his theory have been most used by later writers. One is the idea of people's beliefs and values (their culture) being an important factor in development: the other is the idea of capitalism as involving a spread of what Weber called 'rational behaviour' so that it becomes the norm of everyday life (see box 1.14).

Box 1.14   *Weber and rationalisation*

Weber's idea of rationalisation is complicated. In part it involves the notions of calculation and planning being applied to all areas of life. Think for example of a small shopkeeper who keeps all the information about the business in his or her head, and has no clear idea of how much profit is being made, but just keeps the household and business monies mixed up together. Then think of another shopkeeper who has expanded the business, installed a microcomputer and knows immediately the state of stock, profit and loss account, cost of wages per hour and uses this information to increase profits. The latter business is more *rationalised* than the first. Its procedures are designed in order to achieve the owner's goal – maximum profit – with the greatest efficiency.

Later theorists picked up these ideas – some for example argued that the change from traditional to modern society, from developed to underdeveloped, involved a change in the way people in the society thought. Some of these ideas were included in the work of writers I have already mentioned. For example, Talcott Parsons (Talcott Parsons, *The Evolution of Societies*, Prentice-Hall, Englewood Cliffs, 1977, edited and introduced by Jackson Toby provides a good account of Parsons' writings over the period 1955–77), and many of those who worked with him placed a great deal of emphasis on the importance of values in determining people's behaviour. This is very clear in the work of David McClelland. Writing in 1966 he said:

Usually, rapid economic growth has been explained in terms of 'external' factors – favorable opportunities for trade, unusual natural resources, or conquests that have opened up new markets or produced internal political stability. But I am interested in the internal factors – in the values and motives men have that lead them to exploit opportunities to take advantage of favorable trade conditions; in short, to shape their own destiny.

(The Achievement Motive in Economic Growth, in Hoselitz, B. F. and Moore, W. E. (eds.), *Industrialisation and Society*, UNESCO-MOUTON, 1966, p. 74.)

This kind of theoretical emphasis has a particular outcome in practice – the problems of underdevelopment, poverty and malnutrition are seen as the result of traditional, non-rational thought. The solution to the development problem, according to this view, lies in educational programmes and technical aid aimed at increasing the 'need for achievement' of the people of the underdeveloped regions.

Summary

In this chapter we took the image of the labour migrant as our starting point. This was to emphasise how we all live our lives in relation to social forces beyond our individual control. It was noted that sociology was founded by thinkers like Saint-Simon and Auguste Comte who were trying to understand the changes which were occurring around them in the early years of the industrial revolution. All sociology has its roots in the attempt to understand social change and development.

In the late nineteenth century, Emile Durkheim tried to explain social change as the result of changes in the bonds of morality. These bonds he called 'social solidarity'. With others, he emphasised processes of social evolution. He thought that the alterations in how societies functioned as organic wholes could be studied scientifically. Ideas such as these found expression in the writings of later modernisation theorists such as Wilbert Moore and Walt Rostow.

In contrast to Durkheim, Max Weber tried to identify what it was in people's religious and ethical beliefs that had enabled societies which started with similar technological endowments to develop in quite different ways. He emphasised the influence of Calvinism on the development of capitalist industrialisation in western Europe. Some of his ideas were explored in more detail in the 1960s by writers such as David McClelland.

Another theme in this chapter was that 'theories' are not

true or false. Rather they can be seen as more or less useful languages with which to discuss problems. By virtue of their inclusion or exclusion of different kinds of information, theories define problems and, to a degree, determine how knowledge is divided into different academic disciplines.

2

Development theory: the light of experience

In this chapter, we are going to look at how modernisation theory was criticised during the 1960s and 1970s in the light of the experience of the many countries in Africa and Asia which became independent during that period, and the experience of the Latin American countries which had become independent much earlier (see box 2.1). The most fundamental objection to modernisation theory was that it assumed 'developing' societies could follow the already developed countries along their well-worn path to development. When experience showed that this was not happening, sociologists began to construct theories which asked, and answered, different kinds of questions. In particular, they asked questions about the history of imperialism and its effects on developing countries. In doing this, they moved the discussion of development away from individual societies taken in isolation. They proposed that each society's development problems could only be understood in relation to its place in a 'world system'.

Box 2.1 *Dates of independence of some countries*

Africa

Angola	1976	Mozambique	1975
Benin	1960	Niger	1960
Chad	1960	Nigeria	1960
Congo	1960	Rwanda	1962
Ghana	1957	Sierra Leone	1961
Ivory Coast	1960	Sudan	1956
Kenya	1963	Tanzania	1961
Malawi	1964	Uganda	1962
Mali	1960	Zimbabwe	1980

Middle East/North Africa

Algeria	1960	Morocco	1956
Jordan	1946	Tunisia	1956
Kuwait	1961	North Yemen	1919
Lebanon	1941	South Yemen	1965
Libya	1951		

South/East Asia and Pacific

Bangladesh	1971	Pakistan	1947
India	1947	Papua New Guinea	1975
Indonesia	1949	Singapore	1959
Kampuchea	1954	Sri Lanka	1948
Laos	1954	Taiwan	1949
Malaysia	1957	Vietnam	1954

South/Central America

Argentina	1810	Mexico	1821
Bolivia	1825	Nicaragua	1838
Brazil	1822	Panama	1903
Colombia	1819	Peru	1821
Cuba	1902	Trinidad	1962
El Salvador	1838	Uruguay	1828
Haiti	1804	Venezuela	1830
Jamaica	1962		

(Source: *Third World Atlas*, Crow, B. and Thomas, A., Open University Press, Milton Keynes, 1983.)

The Limits of Modernisation

By the late 1960s it became apparent that these two broad traditions – the Durkheimian and the Weberian – did not adequately explain processes of change taking place in the area now being called variously 'the less developed countries', 'the undeveloped countries' or the 'Third World'.

The newly independent states in Africa and Asia had been expected to proceed in an orderly way to economic growth and parliamentary democracy. Military coups, one party states, deepening poverty in many countries, the war in Vietnam, led to a widely accepted conclusion that the most influential sociological analyses were inadequate. They did not explain what was actually happening in the Third World; neither did they explain the continuing failure of the developed countries to cater for the needs of all their citizens or to achieve their own steady economic growth and development. Concern turned from trying to find ways forward to 'development'. Now the problem was to explain the persistence of poverty in a world where some people were very rich indeed and others barely survived. There was a 'rediscovery' of poverty in Europe and North America (see box 2.2).

Box 2.2 *Poverty and affluence*

For many people in Britain, the 1960s was a period of considerable affluence, it was the time of the 'swinging sixties'. Yet research on the extent of poverty in the United Kingdom attempted to show through the idea of **relative deprivation** that considerable relative poverty continued to exist despite apparent affluence. Poverty came to be seen as not just a matter of basic survival but also to do with deficiency in resources that significantly hampers or prevents participation in social events that give life meaning – quite ordinary things like not being able to have birthday parties, go to the cinema, or visit a disco. This emphasised that poverty is not necessarily the result of any general lack of goods and services in a society, but rather reflects the distribution of these goods and services.

The Royal Commission on the Distribution of Income and Wealth (Cmnd 7595, HMSO, 1979, known as the Diamond Report), collected a lot of evidence about the situation in the 1960s and early 1970s. It showed that in the United Kingdom, a highly developed country, there was also a high degree of inequality.

The top 10 per cent of earners took 23 per cent of all income, while the top 1 per cent of wealth owners owned 27.6 per cent of all wealth.

(Diamond Report, 1979, pp. 15 and 80.)

The Rediscovery of Marxist Sociology

Faced with these difficulties in understanding both developed and underdeveloped societies, sociologists rediscovered another source of social thought which had been ignored in Western sociology. This is the tradition based on the idea of Karl Marx (1818–1883) and Friedrich Engels (1820–1895) as well as some other Marxist thinkers like Leon Trotsky (1879–1940), Vladimir Lenin (1870–1924) and Mao Tse-tung (1893–1976).

It was curious that these had been ignored, because the thoughts of the first two, and the actions of the others, had actually brought about major social change and improvement in the material conditions of millions of people. One reason for the relative invisibility of their thought to the mainstream of Western sociologists was the Cold War; another was that their thought was critical of just the conception of capitalist modernity which was the end point and goal of existing sociological theory. Here we have an example of how social theory can be unacceptable because of the general political and cultural climate at a particular time. During the Cold War, it had been difficult for American theorists to draw upon the traditions of 'the other side'.

An important additional reason for the rediscovery of the Marxist tradition in the sociology of development was undoubtedly that, after 1956, sociologists and social anthropologists were increasingly working and travelling in the new independent countries. Here they met and talked to the educated members of those societies, and learned from them. They heard that in the struggles for independence many Third World intellectuals had found Marxist theories providing better explanations and guides to action than the competing Western product – modernisation theory.

Marx and Engels

Marx and Engels lived in the nineteenth century and confronted the same problems which Durkheim and Weber had tried to tackle. In contrast to these thinkers, however, they argued that the processes of social change and development were in their nature not gradual and evolutionary. Rather they were characterised by conflict of interests between classes in society. The core of these conflicts, called contradictions, was the lack of fit between what a society could produce with its human and technological potential, and the social relations of production which prevented that potential from being realised. This can be seen as a disjunction between the productive potential of a society and the distribution of goods and services among its members. One way in which this theory is important is in its view that social change arises out of political struggles, radical and sudden breaks in continuity, rather than from gradual evolution. For example, groups of people with common interests derived from their position in production (e.g. as wage workers) have to organise to bring about the ends that they want. This conflict is called class struggle, and for Marxists it is seen as the motor of social change and development.

From this basic approach many things followed, but one in particular is important for us. This is the nature of the empires which the European powers had conquered. Lenin and others developed the idea that empires were not benign political outgrowths of European civilisation. Instead, imperialism was an exploitative system of economic, social and political relations which, while changing the colonised societies economically, socially and culturally, changed them in order that they could provide cheap inputs to production in the capitalist societies as well as markets for their products. This arrangement always worked to the advantage of the imperial power. Such an approach to the question of development differs in many ways from those that we have already looked at. But I want to point out one important difference (box 2.3).

Box 2.3   *Imperialism in Africa*

This extract describes imperialism in Africa in a way which is consistent with a Marxian theory. You should notice that it distinguishes between the different effects of imperialism in various regions:

'. . . the imperialist invasion found . . . (Africa) . . . at varying stages of development. By the nineteenth century . . . (West African) . . . peasants produced a number of commodity crops, including coffee, groundnuts, ginger, and had done a brisk trade with Europe for some time. This enabled the imperialists to subordinate local farming to their own interests by monopolising the trading and marketing operations of the African. . . .'

'[In East Africa] peasant production constituted a mainly closed and natural economy. A substantial number of tribes led a nomadic existence. Trade with Europe was only weakly developed and carried on through Arab merchants. . . . In order to obtain raw materials of the necessary type and quantity, intervention was needed. A solution was needed to the same problem as in West Africa, but in this case it could only be solved by expropriating the land, organising European plantations and turning the local population into workers on those plantations. . . . In the Belgian Congo, the policy of the imperialists was initially determined by rubber. To make the Africans gather rubber, it was necessary to confiscate their land and drive them into the jungle by force.'

(Nzula, A. T., et. al., *Forced Labour in Colonial Africa*, Zed Press, 1979, pp. 38–40. Originally published in 1933.)

Marxian theory does not distinguish between the 'scientific' expert sociologist and the policy maker and politician. Indeed, it argues that such a distinction is irrelevant because theory and practice are two sides of the same coin, developing in very close relation with each other. In other words, the 'theoretical language' of Marxist theory must relate very closely to, even be developed out of, the experience of the people who are exploited and oppressed in their everyday lives (see box 2.4). So, if you want to develop a theory about labour migration, you don't just sit in your office. You go out and study the experience of the labour migrants, listen to their stories, become involved in their struggles, and incorporate all that experience into your theory, which is both a social and political theory.

Box 2.4 *Marxism and science*

Marxist thought has a different theory of science from positivists such as Durkheim and his intellectual heirs. From a marxist perspective, social theory cannot be objective. This is because (a) society is characterised by class conflict, and (b) the dominant ideas (and theories) are the ideas of the ruling class. It follows from this that in the process of class struggle, opposing groups will develop their own theories. These theories will provide them with a language suitable to the needs and problems they face from their position in society. This view of social theory is called 'praxis' – the unity of theory and practice. It contrasts with the positivist view of social science which says that the social world can be studied as though it is a 'thing'.

Although Marx himself did not do this, some other Marxists have. For example, when Mao Tse-tung (who led the Chinese revolution in the 1930s and 1940s) wanted to understand the peasants in China he went to the rural area of Hunan and wrote a report derived from what he saw and what they told him. This differs from the research method of many sociologists and social anthropologists who, until quite recently, used their visits to 'the field' to test the theories which they or others had constructed beforehand. Such a view of how and why social research should be done arises because all of these people were involved in very practical political action. Hence their insistence on the close relation between intellectual analysis and political action, between theory and political practice.

In 1967 this tradition of Marxist thought began to attract a wider interest among sociologists and others interested in development. In an article with the provocative title 'The Sociology of Development and the Underdevelopment of Sociology', a German–American economist living in Latin America attacked the whole of the then dominant modernisation theory. In no uncertain terms this writer, A. G. Frank, dismissed the theories as useless from a policy point of view because they failed to define correctly the kinds of social and economic processes at work in the underdeveloped countries. In later work, he went on to support these assertions with detailed historical case studies of Chile and Brazil. Drawing on the Marxian tradition and on the theories which Latin American economists and sociologists had developed to explain the problems of their societies, he argued that for ideological reasons Western sociology had incorrectly defined the problem as one of 'development'. To pose the problem in this way assumed that development could occur in any society if it adopted the right economic policies along with a work ethic and parliamentary democracy. Frank said that this was not possible. Instead of development being possible, what was actually in train was a process of underdevelopment. You should note that he gave this word a new meaning. He meant that rather than relations between rich and poor nations being beneficial to the latter, they should be seen as positively destructive of them, hindering and distorting their development. Underdevelopment is not a stage which precedes development, rather it now has to be seen as the end result of imperialism and colonialism. Another term, 'undevelopment', was introduced to describe societies which had simple technology but were unaffected by the developed societies. This view of development and underdevelopment sees both states as the result of interaction between societies (see box 2.5).

Box 2.5   *The thesis of capitalist underdevelopment*

In his study of Latin America, Frank argued that underdevelopment is the result of capitalist development. Writing of Chile, and using the Marxian concept of contradiction, he said:

'. . . underdevelopment in Chile is the necessary product of four centuries of capitalist development and of the internal contradictions of capitalism itself. These contradictions are the expropriation of economic surplus from the many and its appropriation by the few, the polarisation of the capitalist system into metropolitan centre and peripheral satellites, and the continuity of the fundamental structure of the capitalist system throughout the history of its expansion and transformation, due to the persistence or re-creation of these contradictions everywhere and at all times. My thesis is that these capitalist contradictions and the historical development of the capitalist system have generated underdevelopment in the peripheral satellites whose economic surplus was expropriated, while generating economic development in the metropolitan centres which appropriate that surplus – and further, that this process still continues.'

(Frank, A. G., *Capitalism and Underdevelopment in Latin America*, Penguin, 1971, p. 27.)

A Committed Sociology of Development

This line of thought made the sociology of development much more critical of the existing relations between rich and poor countries. It raised questions as to whether or not the best path to development would be revolution or complete withdrawal from the world system of social, political and economic relations. It also posed uncomfortable questions about the relations between different parts of the same society, not only in the Third World but, for example, between the wealthy south east of Britain and the poorer north.

Frank, and others who were in broad agreement with him, became known as the Dependency Theorists. Their work raised the question of development in a new way. In particular, it meant the sociologist could no longer look at 'them' and wonder how to bring about 'their' development. It had to take 'our' development into account in explaining 'their' underdevelopment. Very importantly, it made sociologists think seriously about the study of history and the role of the past in understanding the present.

In some respects, however, dependency theory gave too easy an explanation. The problems of the Third World could now be explained as the outcome of exploitation by the developed world. But internal factors such as natural resource shortages, class exploitation and population growth could be too easily dismissed. To this extent it encouraged both a degree of utopianism – everything would be all right if dependency was done away with – and also a degree of pessimism – if dependency cannot be done away with, then there is nothing that politicians, policy makers or people could do. While dependency theory appeared to provide a simple and powerful model of the origins and nature of underdevelopment, it failed to confront some very important questions which had been central to modernisation theory. In particular, it did not really give sufficient weight to the role of culture and ideas in development. You will recall how, under the influence of Weber, modernisation theory asked what part religious beliefs played. Questions like this remain absent from dependency theory. In addition, it has been said that dependency theory is too general – it does not distinguish sufficiently between the histories and circumstances of different countries. As you can see from the example in box 2.3, in Africa the precise impact of imperialism varied. It depended on what form of social and economic organisation existed there prior to colonialism.

The Warren Thesis

One response to dependency theory has come from within Marxism. It is rooted in Marx's view that development would have to take a capitalist form, destroying non-capitalist societies in order to allow for their reconstruction first along capitalist lines, and then socialist. Marx, in his scattered writings on India in the nineteenth century, railed against what he saw as the static and deeply conservative nature of oriental society.

Bill Warren, writing in 1980 (Warren, B., *Imperialism: Pioneer of Capitalism*, Verso, 1980) equally railed against what he considered the utopianism of dependency theory. He said that it was a product of the period of decolonisation, and was part of the nationalist ideologies which had gone along with the independence movements. It served as an excuse for the existence of poverty and backwardness in the Third World, placing the blame on the developed countries. It therefore failed to notice that capitalist development had actually been taking place in many parts of the Third World. For example in Egypt, Argentina and Brazil it can be argued that manufacturing industry is as important in the economy as it is in the United States and Canada (Warren, 1980, p. 245). He also said that dependency theory did not recognise that there were many reasons internal to Third World societies which held them back (see box 2.6). Here he was thinking of the absence of entrepreneurship (which Weber and McClelland had thought very important), and cultural patterns, such as the seclusion of women.

Box 2.6 *Warren on capitalist development*

Warren argues that:

'1. Contrary to current marxist views [by which he means dependency theory] . . . evidence suggests that the prospects for successful capitalist development in many underdeveloped countries are quite favourable.

2. . . . evidence further shows that substantial advances along these lines have already been achieved, especially in industrialisation. . . .

3. Direct colonialism, far from having retarded or distorted indigenous capitalist development ... acted as a powerful engine of progressive social change ... both by its destructive effects on pre-capitalist social systems and by its implantation of the elements of capitalism. ...

4. Insofar as there are obstacles to ... development, they originate not in current relationships between imperialism and the Third World, but in the internal contradictions of the Third World itself.'

(Warren, B., 1980, pp. 9–10.)

Barrington Moore

Another development theorist who stands apart from dependency theory is Barrington Moore. A historian, he examined the history of a number of different countries – Britain, France, the USA, Japan and China – and concluded that there had been different routes to development. In his view there were three routes. These are:

1. *bourgeois democratic revolution*, led by a strong indigenous middle class, which resulted in capitalist democracy in Britain, France and the USA;

2. *fascist revolution*, as in Germany and Japan where, because the middle class with its entrepreneurial skills was weak, capitalism came about through an authoritarian state;

3. *peasant revolution leading to communism*, as in Russia and China, where centralised monarchies stifled the impulse to capitalist development, and the way forward had depended on an uprising by the mass of peasants led by intellectuals.

Moore differs from both Marxism and modernisation theory, but uses ideas from both. For him, development is predominantly an internal process, and the result depends on the relative power of social classes. The two main classes with which he is concerned are indicated by the title of his book, *The Social Origins of Dictatorship and Democracy: lord and peasant in the making of the modern world* (Penguin, 1966).

World System Theory

This type of theory is also rooted in Marxism. It is a development of dependency theory, but differs from it inasmuch as it pays considerable attention to the specific histories of different regions of the world, and does not generalise in quite the same way.

Once it could be said that the problems of underdevelopment were the result of historical relationships of exploitation between the developed and underdeveloped societies, the whole perspective altered. It seemed that development could not any longer be thought of as a problem faced by separate societies; no society was totally unaffected by the development of a world economic and social system. Although this view was not new it was restated clearly in the writings of Immanuel Wallerstein. In his book *The Modern World System: capitalist agriculture and the origins of the European world economy in the sixteenth century* (Academic Press, New York, 1974), Wallerstein says:

. . . I abandoned the idea altogether of taking either the sovereign state or that vaguer concept, the national society, as the unit of analysis. I decided that neither one was a social system and that one could only speak of social change in social systems. The only system in this scheme was the world-system.

(Wallerstein, I., 1974, p. 7.)

World system theories (Wallerstein is not alone, and there are variants, notably Samir Amin and Frank in his later writing) provide a theoretical language which combines sociological conflict theory with economic and historical data considered on a world scale. It analyses particular problems of development and underdevelopment in terms of their history, sociology and economics, and in the light of the broadest happenings in a world society, in particular the development of capitalism. In this view of things, the labour migrant with whom we began is not alone. The 'otherness' which labour migrants experience can now be seen as the outcome of their location within long term historical changes taking place throughout the world.

Peasants and the World System

There is one other development of sociological theory which we must be aware of. This was a response to some of the problems which were apparent in dependency theory. You may recall that I suggested that dependency theory was too general. It has been accused of being so general that it explains nothing. A response to this was to try to look at some of the detail of social systems in the Third World and to explain how it was that, within a 'capitalist' system of exploitative relationships between societies, some societies seemed to be able to survive whilst producing in ways which were not in the least bit capitalist. These different 'modes of production', such as small scale peasant farming or pastoralism, were clearly not capitalist, they did not depend on wage labourers working for an employer or on private ownership of land. What were they? How did they fit into the relations of dependency between societies?

The answer provided was that they contributed to the continuation and growth of capitalism by providing very cheap inputs to capitalist production (see box 2.7).

Box 2.7 *Peasants in Colombia*

Michael Taussig studied the relationship between small scale peasant agriculture and large scale capitalist plantations in the Cauca Valley, Colombia. He concluded:

In the evolution of the relationship between large-scale capitalist farming and peasant production, the former is less efficient than the latter on several crucial criteria. But because of its monopoly over land, capitalist farming compensates for its inefficiencies by being able to take advantage of peasant efficiencies . . . it is by reducing peasant farm size below a certain minimum that gives to the capitalist class the mechanism for accumulating surplus. In other words, bigness and technology are not in themselves inherently more efficient; rather they provide the muscle necessary to coerce a laboour force into being, as well as the discipline and authority necessary to extract surplus value from that labour.

(Taussig, M., Peasant Economics and the Development of Capitalist Agriculture in the Cauca Valley, Colombia, in Harriss, J. C. (ed.), *Rural Development*, Hutchinson, 1982, p. 181.)

Peasant producers, for example, do not calculate the precise cost of their work. They are said to work as hard and as long as is required to meet their survival needs. If the prices for their products fall, they work a bit longer, they don't make a precise calculation as to whether or not it is worth their while in terms of a profit. If market conditions become very adverse, they can, in theory, withdraw completely from producing for the market, and fall back on a basic level of subsistence production. But, as long as peasant producers remain associated with and part of a world system, then they provide various forms of cheap inputs to capitalist production – whether those inputs are cheap labour or cheap cotton.

The Peasants as a Special Kind of Economy

Sociologists (and economists) have interpreted these peasant economies as being very efficient. There is considerable evidence that this is so. Peasant farmers are not 'primitive' and inefficient. Rather, they have a detailed knowledge of their own agriculture and, because of their need to survive, use a great deal of labour per unit of land.

On this evidence, a particular 'school' of sociologists has argued that future agricultural development policy in the Third

World should emphasise the small peasant farmer as against large scale, capital intensive agriculture. This view has a long history, going back to some Russian economists in the 1880s and summed up in the work of Alexander Chayanov (writing between 1912 and 1937), and has come to be known as 'populism'. It is of importance because it questions whether industrialisation is the main path to economic development. It also asks whether capital intensive agriculture is really appropriate for many parts of the world. Populist theory directs attention to the way capital intensive strategies imposed by governments 'organise' and plan the lives of rural people, restricting their freedom of choice with respect to production decisions. These restrictions cause them to resist government in various ways, because they feel that they are being exploited (see box 2.8).

Box 2.8 *Governments and peasants*

In this extract, Gavin Williams is concerned to show how a revolution made by urban intellectuals can end up exploiting the peasants, and in so doing, threaten the very basis of the revolution by evoking peasant opposition and thus a fall in food production. This sequence of events happened in the Soviet Union after their revolution in 1917. It has also happened in many African countries, notably in Ethiopia since 1974.

'... revolutionary victory may give the 'petty bourgeoisie' control of the institutions of state power which they alone are capable of directing, thus ending their reliance on the masses. Hence the need to avoid taking over the institutions of a centralised ... state, with its capital, presidential palace, concentrated ministries, and the authoritarian chain of command. In economic policy, the priority must be given to raising food production. This cannot be achieved by state direction of peasant producers, but only by encouraging peasant initiative based on their own experience and improving their own material well-being, and defending their own gains against the demands even of the revolutionary state.'

(Williams, G. P., Taking the Part of Peasants, in Harriss, J. C., (ed.), 1982, p. 381.)

Williams argues this case because he thinks that if peasants are not exploited they will retain incentives to produce food. It is interesting to note that in recent years the World Bank (which funds many agricultural development projects in the Third World) has adopted the view that funding peasant agriculture is often an efficient strategy for development in Third World circumstances.

Sociology, Development and Sociological Theory

Where does this leave us? We can now see the labour migrant's journey in a new light. In moving to this new perspective, the sociology of development has itself undergone a considerable process of development. In part this is because it has ceased to be so narrow and has begun to take into consideration both history and the experience of ordinary people in their struggle to survive and change their world. But major problems remain.

One problem which may have struck you in the last few pages is that, in a strange way, and despite the inclusion of many of the ideas of Marxist sociology both in world system theory as well as in dependency theory, there is a subtle kind of functionalism. The world system is composed of parts which make it work in a particular way, enabling the spread and development of capitalism.

Perhaps this is a feature of scientific thought. Once you define the boundaries of your system, as Wallerstein had to do, then inevitably you explain how it works, and all the parts of that whole must, by definition, contribute to the continuation of the system which you began by defining. This is a circular argument which it is difficult to find a way out of. It has to do with the way in which we think about problems in any science. The danger it presents is that we may forget that the 'system' we analyse is something we thought up at our own particular conjunction of biography and history. If we do forget that, we face the danger of moving from the use of a theoretical language which is *more or less useful*, to saying that the 'system' is a 'true' account, and worse, that it tells us what is right and wrong.

Despite its limitations, and subtle functionalism, current sociology of development theory remains critical of the circumstances which produce poverty and hardship for most of the world's population and locates the origins of those problems within the struggle for resources between the First World and the Third World, and between groups within the societies of those worlds.

Summary

In this chapter, we have seen how the Marxian strand in development theory leads in a number of directions, emphasising development and underdevelopment as the result of interaction between societies and their environments. Imperialism has been the focus of such theories. Over the last fifteen years, the most influential approaches have been dependency theory and world system theory, both reactions against modernisation theory. However, from within the Marxist tradition there has in turn been criticism of these, notably by Warren.

Part Two

TOWN
AND
COUNTRYSIDE

3

Urbanisation and urbanism

In this chapter we look at the ways in which sociologists and social anthropologists have tried to understand the growth of towns – urbanisation, and the nature of social life in towns – urbanism.

While it is true that there have been urban settlements in various human societies for something like the past 5000 years, not all towns were or are alike; their quality of 'townness' is often the result of very different influences. While it is probably obvious that ancient Rome and modern London are different – although we may not be able to define the differences very precisely – the differences between Lagos (Nigeria) and Paris might not be so easy to describe.

When sociologists look at towns, they are, broadly speaking, interested in two sets of related problems. These are:

1. the social and economic reasons for the development of towns in particular places;

2. the types of social relation that characterise towns.

If we look at these ideas in more detail we will see first of all what is specific about the sociological approach, and secondly how the sociology of development deals with these problems from its particular perspective.

In one sense, when we look at the reasons for the development of a town, we are asking questions about its biography, its history. You may have been taught in geography lessons that big towns like Manchester developed because natural resources were nearby, and these could be processed using the available technology so as to produce cotton goods. That kind of explanation would only be the very beginning of a sociological explanation. It leaves unanswered questions such as: Why did that technology become available and profitable to use at that time?

Why was there a demand for cotton goods? Why were there people available to work in the mills? What had they been doing before? How were they persuaded to stop what they had been doing? . . . and so on. In other words, what general social and economic changes were occurring which led to the establishment of the British textile industry at that time and in that place?

What about the second question? One way to answer it is to divide it into two parts, the large scale and the very small scale. In the first part we can consider the physical use of space by different social groups; in the second part we can ask how the people in the town go about explaining to themselves and others the meaning of their lives. You should think here about the rather special use of the word '**meaning**' in the sociology of Max Weber. Remember that Weber emphasises the influence which people's beliefs have on their social action. If you think about that, you will see that it leads to an intermediate point between the physical use of space and the individual's beliefs – to the forms of organisation which people adopt in towns, their households, clubs, religious bodies and political groups. These three positions – historical, cultural and organisational – provide us with a framework for talking about the urbanisation process in development.

Two main traditions have been influential. The first of these has its roots in the sociology of Emile Durkheim and also in that of Ferdinand Tonnies – both of whom you may recall placed great emphasis on that favourite ninteenth century problem, the loss of community. Although this was a nineteenth century problem, it remains with us in different forms today – not least of all because of the way in which we experience the 'otherness' and apparent impersonality of society as it impinges upon us. Some people think that 'inner-city problems' are in part the result of loss of community.

This tradition of urban sociology developed a body of quite sophisticated theory in the United States of America in the 1920s and 1930s. It came to be known as the Chicago School. The main theorists were Louis Wirth (1897–1952), himself an immigrant, and Robert Park (1864–1944), and one of its most interesting pieces of research was done by F. Zorbaugh, and reported in his book *The Goldcoast and the Slum*.

The main problem which concerned this school was that of social order in a society of immigrants – the processes of *integration* and *assimilation* of hosts of strangers into the great American cities. The main organising concepts of this approach were: the urban subculture – the systems of meaning which the immigrant communities and class communities of Chicago and Detroit developed for themselves – and the manner in which the social distinctions of the city were reflected in the way that different subcultures and classes lived in different parts of cities. Although the mainstream of research in urbanization in the Third World does not have its roots in this American tradition, it borrows some of their ideas such as *subculture*, assimilation and integration.

Urbanisation and Social Order

The major influences on the study of urbanisation are Durkheim and Tonnies. Sociological problems reflect not only the 'purely' academic interests of the researcher, they are also related to broader social problems. City government and administration requires knowledge of what is going on among the people. And where many of those urban people are newcomers, those who are responsible for the orderly running of the city will require sociological information to help them understand and control the social problems of the growing city. In some superficial respects, the sociological problems of Chicago were the same as those to be found in Kuala Lumpur, Buenos Aires or Cape Town. It was this apparent similarity which led to the application of modernisation theory to urbanisation. The argument is set out in box 3.1.

Box 3.1 *Industrialisation and urbanisation*

Industrialisation is a core feature of the process of economic development; the evidence of western European and North American development suggests that industrialisation, urbanisation and development are in some way related. In the developed countries, urbanisation and industrialisation have been catalysts for later processes of rural development. They have led to a modernisation of agriculture, an improvement of rural life and a linking of the rural areas into an integrated system of production and consumption with the urban industrial centres.

An important feature of this view is that it takes as one of its major assumptions the idea that 'development' flows outwards from the city, and that the rural areas are waiting there to be developed. This view is known as 'dualism' because it assumes that two economic and social systems – the urban and the rural, the developed and the underdeveloped – exist side by side and have to be stitched together through a process of modernisation and development. It reflects a particular view of what was going on in many colonial societies. It was a view from the perspective of the colonial rulers. One of their main concerns was how to have enough labour for the needs of the new industries without having so much labour that the city would be unable to cope, or the new city dwellers might constitute a threat to order. This worry continues in many Third World countries today, but reached its most explicit form in the Republic of South Africa where the ideology of government is dominated by concern with 'influx control' which has become the basis of the apartheid policy.

Colonial governments saw labour migration as a major social problem. Thus, much of the work undertaken by sociologists and social anthropologists during the 1940s and later focused on the ways in which labour migrants became integrated or assimilated into urban life.

The main developments in this field took place among a group of sociologists and social anthropologists working at the Rhodes–Livingstone Institute in what is now Zambia, during the 1940s and 1950s. Their work focused on two sets of related

processes: the effects of labour migration on the social structure
of the sending communities and the ways in which the migrants
adjusted to life in the towns. Watson, in his study of the
Mambwe people, *Tribal Cohesion in a Money Economy*, examined
the changes which labour migration brought about in Mambwe
social organisation, and in particular the organisation of
production. Audrey Richards in her study of the Bemba people,
Land, Labour and Diet in Northern Rhodesia, showed that withdrawal of young men from the local economy had resulted in
a terrible decline in production, and thus to rural poverty and
starvation.

At the other end of the migration process, J. C. Mitchell
studied the social organisation of labour migrants in towns. In
his classic essay *The Kalela Dance*, he showed that while labour
migrants referred to each other by tribal labels, these had
different meanings in town than they had at home in the
countryside. They had become a kind of shorthand to sum
up cultural differences within the migrant population. They
provided mental maps of urban social differences. However,
while labour migrants may identify themselves as 'Bemba',
'Mambwe', 'Indian', 'Pakistani' or 'Irish', they are also all
workers, and can also be analysed using the concept of class.
In box 3.2, Valdo Pons tells us something about this in colonial
times in the Belgian Congo.

Box 3.2   *Tribe and class in the colonial city: Zaire*

In this extract, Valdo Pons sums up the problem of conceptual-
ising social division when studying urbanisation in Africa. He
invites us to consider the relative importance of 'tribe' and
'class'. Writing in 1969 about research that he did in the 1950s,
he says:

'The initial questions which struck me concerning "tribalism"
and "class" in Stanleyville can be explained very simply by
imagining two observers being conducted on casual visits to two
different neighbourhoods in the town. One observer could well
have been taken to an area where there was a marked tendency

for members of the same tribe to live next to each other. Most of his observations here would have suggested the existence of discrete tribal neighbourhoods each with a relatively self-sufficient social life. . . . The second observer could, however, have been taken to a neighbourhood where there was no readily discernible evidence of ethnic residential concentration, and where members of many different tribes lived side by side and commonly shared the same dwelling-compounds, and sometimes the same houses. Here he would have heard most inhabitants conversing in one or both of the *linguae francae* of Swahili and Lingala . . . and he would have seen people mixing in public places . . . he would have discovered that in this area the incidence of non-tribal marriages was high and that informal friendship groups . . . consisted of members of different tribes. . . . We are thus naturally led to enquire into the nature of these variations and . . . to ask . . . how the two principles of "tribalism" and "class" operated simultaneously within the same community.'

(Pons, V., *Stanleyville*, Oxford University Press, 1969, pp. 6–7.)

This important question is discussed in relation to Britain by another writer, Eric Hobsbawm, who says:

'All national working classes tend to be heterogeneous, and with multiple identifications. . . . An Indian shop steward in Slough may see himself for one purpose as a member of the British working class . . . for another as a coloured person . . . for another as an Indian . . . for another as a Sikh . . . as a Punjabi. . . . Of course some of these identifications, however important for everyday purposes (e.g. arranging the marriage of sons and daughters), are politically subordinate.'

(Hobsbawm, E. J., *Worlds of Labour*, Weidenfield and Nicholson, 1984, p. 49.)

What both writers are talking about is the relation between class (position in production) and cultural (religious and ethnic) factors in social life. This is an important, and fascinating problem in all sociology.

This tradition of studying urbanisation as part of the development process focused on the ways labour migrants were assimilated or integrated into urban life. Many detailed and informative community studies came out of this school of research, such as that by Valdo Pons, and Philip Mayer's *Townsmen or Tribesmen: conservatism and the process of urbanisation in a South African city* (Oxford University Press, Capetown, 1971) which examined the development of social differences among people coming from the same rural area to work in the town, and the way in which some of them tried very hard to maintain their traditions while others emphasised that they were educated and 'modern', 'school' people – different ways of giving life meaning in a strange environment (see box 3.3).

Box 3.3   *Reds, rascals and gentlemen in South Africa*

In a study of a small rural settlement in South Africa, O'Connell shows how the labour migration has brought some of these cultural differences back to the rural areas. He talks about three groups of people, all of the Xesibe tribe, but very different in their culture because of their different responses to urban life. The three groups are:

'Reds . . . who cling to the traditional way of life . . . in Xhosa they are called *abantu ababomvu* (Red people) . . . a reference to the traditional custom of smearing red ochre in the hair, on the body and over clothing. . . . Reds generally spend childhood and early adolescence herding stock . . . (their) school experience is short, and they are never fully incorporated into the school world. They live according to norms which are firmly rooted in their ancestral religion. Their . . . behaviour is determined by tradition . . . reflected in their respect for parental authority, a keen interest in livestock, fighting, traditional dancing and music, beer drinking and sacrifices. . . .'

' "Rascal" is a . . . translation of the term *iindlavini* or wine drinker. . . . Reds think of School (educated) people, Rascals and Gentlemen, as traitors. . . . Rascals join an organisation

---

called *ilitye* (stone) when they have completed an initial labour contract. *Ilitye* . . . is a paramilitary organisation and Rascals do . . . spend much of their time quarrelling with Rascals from other parts of the district. . . . Rascals . . . look and act like School people in some respects, and like traditionalists in others. . . .'

' "Gentlemen" is a translation of the Xhosa *amanene* . . . they detest what they consider the common habits, rustic manners and traditional inclinations of the Reds and Rascals, and think of themselves as civilised by comparison . . . their social life centres around the school, church and the bars in the nearby towns . . . owing to their educational qualifications, they have more opportunity to pick and choose the work they do. . . .'

(O'Connell, M. C., *Xesibe Reds, Rascals and Gentlemen at Home and at Work*, in Mayer, P. (ed.) *Black Villagers in an Industrial Society*, Oxford University Press, Capetown, 1980, pp. 257–260.)

Most of these studies used the concepts of integration and assimilation in order to understand how strangers became part of an existing and dominant urban society (see box 3.4). A criticism which can be levelled at them is that they fail to give sufficient weight to the city as a place in which the migrants have their own views of the future, want to pursue their own interests, and in Marx's words will 'make their own history'.

Box 3.4 *Assimilation and integration*

The concepts of assimilation and integration were also important in another, but related field of sociology, the sociology of race relations in the United Kingdom, where, for example, Patterson's study of Caribbean migrants to the United Kingdom in the 1950s (*Dark Strangers*, Tavistock, 1963) also emphasised 'integration' and 'assimilation'. In the United States, a related view of the problems was also developing. This emphasises the continuing 'culture of poverty' and deprivation in the shanty towns of Central and South America. Oscar Lewis's graphic reportage of day to day life in these slums, for example in his book *La Vida* (Secker and Warburg, 1967), provides a tragic picture of social disorder and deprivation.

Urbanisation and Modernisation

This body of community studies was not clearly located within any wider framework of theory. Friedmann (*Regional Development Policy: a case study of Venezuela*, MIT Press, Boston, 1966), tried to draw together the assumptions which supported this type of work. Working within a modernisation perspective, he identified four stages in the evolution of a city (see box 3.5).

Box 3.5 *Evolution of the city*

1. The early period of colonisation: many independent rural communities supporting themselves by subsistence production.

2. The establishment of a few industries, mines and plantations together with an urban centre for their administration. The emergence of a dualistic social, economic and spatial structure, with gross regional inequalities in income and services. Emergence of a 'primate' city.

3. Spread of industrial production and 'modern' farming. Political opposition from the regions focused around the issues of regional inequity. This provokes the central government to undertake regional development policies in order to rectify the imbalance. A wider spread of economic development occurs.

4. In the final stage a fully integrated society and economy develops, in which rural–urban inequality is not very pronounced and in which political and cultural integration has been achieved.

There were a number of problems with Friedmann's theory:

1. It assumed that the initial colonial intervention took place for the good of the local population, and that the colonised areas were sparsely populated and characterised by small scale subsistence societies awaiting development. Such a view may reflect some features of the colonial experience, but certainly not the majority of cases – India, Ghana and Peru hardly fit into this view of the pre-colonial situation.

2. This view seriously underestimated the role of foreign interests in assuming that regional interests could affect central policy – particularly when those central, urban interests were more likely to be those of the colonising foreign power than of the colonised people.

3. The model is largely apolitical, failing to recognise that the politics of regional and urban development would have been largely dominated by the colonisers and, to a lesser extent, by those members of the local urban elite who benefited from colonialism.

4. Poverty is seen as the result of technical problems of distribution, rather than the outcome of group and class action aimed at keeping down the wage level in the towns, and the costs of agricultural products in the countryside.

5. Perhaps the greatest limitation of the theory is that which it derives from modernisation theory in general – the assumption that urban development in the Third World will follow the same path as was assumed to have occurred in the now developed countries.

The Marxian Analysis of Urbanisation

The alternative tradition within which sociologists have studied the problems of urban life stems from Marxism, with its emphasis on class relations, conflict, contradiction and exploitation. Looking at the process using these concepts produces a very different account of urban and regional development.

The remote origin of this approach can be detected in one particular piece of nineteenth century writing on urbanisation. This is Engels' *The Condition of the Working Class in England* (Blackwell, 1958), a study of Manchester written in 1844. In this remarkable study, Engels shows how working class life in early nineteenth century Manchester had to be understood in relation to:

the expansion of commerce and industry, the conquest of virtually all unprotected foreign markets, the rapid expansion of capital and national wealth.

(Engels, F., 1958, p. 15.)

These changes involved the workers in towns losing their ownership of tools and capital and their descent into a terrible poverty which stood in stark contrast to the wealth which they were instrumental in creating. For Engels, urban poverty was just one aspect of the overall relations between classes during a period of capitalist development. The picture he paints of working class conditions resembles an account of life in the shanty towns of the Third World today (see box 3.6). He says:

The vast majority of the inhabitants of the great towns are workers. . . . The workers do not possess any property and nearly all live from hand to mouth on their wages. Society having degenerated into a collection of selfish individuals, no one bothers about the workers and their families . . . the most highly-skilled worker is therefore continually threatened with the loss of his livelihood and that means death by starvation. . . . The working class quarters of the towns are always badly laid out. Their houses are jerry-built and are kept in a bad state of repair. They are badly ventilated, damp and unhealthy. . . . The clothing of the workers is also normally inadequate and many workers go about clad in rags. The workers' diet is generally poor and often almost inedible.

(Engels, F., 1958, pp. 86–87.)

Box 3.6 *La Esmeralda, Puerto Rico*

There are many terms for the slums inhabited by the poor of the Third World. In Africa they may be called 'shanty towns', 'cardboard cities' (Sudan); in Latin America 'favelas', 'barrios'; in North Africa 'bidonville' (towns built out of 'bidons', tin cans); in India 'bustees'. Oscar Lewis describes one as follows:

'Even though La Esmeralda is only ten minutes away from the Governor's Palace and the heart of San Juan, it is physically and socially marginal to the city. The wall above it stands as a kind of symbol separating it from the city. . . . From the wall down to the sea, the physical condition of the houses becomes poorer and poorer, and the social status of the people grows correspondingly lower, until on the beach itself the poorest people live in the most dilapidated houses. To live on the beach is dangerous, for there is the constant threat of a high tide which may wipe out the houses. . . . The beach is also the dirtiest part of La Esmeralda. Several large conduits, broken in places, carry sewage down to the sea, and the beach swarms with flies and is littered with trash – garbage, human feces, beer bottles, condoms, broken beds and rotten pieces of wood. . . . Nevertheless, the people of La Esmeralda use the beach for bathing, for love-making, for fishing and, when hungry, for collection of snails and crabs. And they raise pigs on the beach because of the abundant supply of garbage.'

(Lewis, O., *La Vida*, Secker and Warburg, 1967, p. 37.)

Engels contrasts this situation with a characteristically romantic nineteenth century account of preindustrial rural life in which:

Wives and daughters spun the yarn, which the men either wove themselves or sold to a weaver. Most of the weavers' families lived in the country near to a town and earned enough to live on. In those days the demand from the local market, which was virtually the only outlet for cloth, was steady and satisfactory.

(Engels, F., 1958, p. 9.)

Recent Marxist theories of urbanisation take as their main problem the broad structural understanding of the Third World city, looking at it within the framework of dependent development and underdevelopment. Rural urban migration is seen as the outcome of policies introduced by colonising powers. These aimed at the transfer of cheap labour from the rural to the urban areas, often through force and coercion. The means employed included compulsory labour and hut and head taxes which had to be paid in cash. Cash which could only be earned from cash crop production, work on settler farms (as in central and southern Africa or parts of Latin America), or from working in the mines or urban industries. The underlying force in the process of urbanisation is seen as the capitalists' need to accumulate capital.

This process is reflected in the spatial organisation of the city, with its wealthy core and its periphery of shanty towns. Regional disparities in income and infrastructure, typically between rural and urban areas, are the outcome of this form of uneven capitalist development in the Third World.

E. Castells (*The Urban Question: a Marxist approach*, Edward Arnold, 1977) provides a model which contrasts with Friedmann's. He identifies three stages in Third World urbanisation (see box 3.7).

Box 3.7 *A model of Third World urbanisation*

Castells' three stages are:

1. During the colonial period, the surplus which is produced in the colony is removed by means of foreign commercial and political control over trade, investment and domestic economic policy. An example of this is discrimination against local industries in favour of products produced by industries in the colonising society – the destruction of the Indian textile industry during the colonial period is an example of this.

2. In this stage, while the country may have become politically independent, surplus is still extracted, notably through unequal

trading arrangements, where foreign companies control the prices of both imports and exports, and manipulate the trade to their advantage.

3. The final stage is a period of monopoly industrial and financial domination, where very large multinational companies, some of which have budgets larger than the states in which they operate, control the large scale manufacturing and agribusiness sectors which may have developed through a web of subsidiary companies with local shareholders, or through banking and other financial arrangements, or through internal accounting procedures such as transfer pricing. At this stage, surplus is extracted by means of profit repatriation, royalty payments and patent licensing.

If we look at urban society from this perspective, the problem is no longer one of 'adjustment', 'assimilation' or 'integration'. Rather it is one of class relations and class politics in the urban environment. Within this theory, social problems such as poverty, inadequate health care, poor nutrition and bad housing become aspects of class relations, issues over which classes fight political battles.

A Theory Which Excludes People?

Marxist interpretations of urban social life and of urbanisation have been criticised as being too *deterministic*. This means that too little weight is attached to the potential for independent action among urban dwellers. While the modernisation approach assumes that governments, both colonial and independent, are basically well meaning if at times technically incompetent, this approach assumes them to be pursuing their own class interests, and holds out little or no hope for effective political action on the part of the rural and urban poor.

There is a curious parallel here with other parts of Marxist theory. You will remember how Engels, in the quotation above, saw urban society as 'a collection of selfish individuals' – an aspect of **'alienation'** which was the concept Marx and Engels used to describe some aspects of the loss of community and of moral certainty which had come to pass with the development of urban industrial society. Durkheim used the concept of **'anomie'** to describe some of the same phenomena. What is important about these observations is the assumed passiveness and ineffectiveness of the urban poor.

There is much evidence that this is not the case, and was not the case in England when Engels was writing. E. P. Thompson in his *The Making of the English Working Class* (Penguin, 1978) shows how in England, the working class took many initiatives, cultural, educational, financial (through mutual aid societies) as well as political (through attempts to form trade unions) – all aimed at improving their lot. Much the same is true of the urban poor in the Third World. The many 'voluntary associations', churches, and social clubs studied by members of the Rhodes–Livingstone Institute as examples of adaptation to city life, can all be seen as forms of organisation which, in the right circumstances, may take on very explicit and powerful political significance. The weight of this statement is demonstrated by Pons' research, which, among other concerns, paid a lot of attention to the various kinds of clubs which urban Africans formed. In the front of the book, which deals mainly with how people become 'urban' and how this can be conceptualised and measured, we find a remarkable picture. It shows the members of the committee of an association of educated Congolese, together with their European president. These people were referred to as 'evolues' – people who had evolved culturally to a level which allowed them restricted access to Belgian colonial society. On the right of the photograph we see Patrice Lumumba, who only a few years later became the first president of the independent Democratic Republic of the Congo!

Class and Culture in Third World Cities

Box 3.8 *Urbanisation in the developing world*

'Developing societies, almost without exception, are increasingly concentrating their populations in urban places. In 1920, 4.8 per cent of the population of Africa, 5.7 per cent of that of South East Asia, 7.2 percent of that of East Asia, and 14.4 per cent of that of Latin America lived in places of 20,000 or more inhabitants; by 1975, the respective percentages were 18.1, 17.4, 23.6 and 40.5. Two traits of this urbanisation deserve attention. First, there is considerable variation between countries and, significantly, between continents of the developing world in both the rate and extent of urbanisation. Second, the increase in urbanisation begins consistently from the mid-nineteenth century onwards, but accelerates, in most countries, in the period following World War II.'

(Roberts, B., Cities in Developing Societies, in Shanin, T. and Alavi, H. (eds.), *Introduction to the Sociology of Developing Societies*, Macmillan, 1982, p. 367.)

Some of the largest cities in the world are in the Third World. Mexico City, probably the largest, has a population of 16 million and may reach 25 million by the end of the century. However, paradoxically, the rate of migration to these cities is slowing down. Indeed, with considerable variation, we can say that on average only 30 per cent of the populations of Third World countries live in cities and this proportion is unlikely to increase before the middle of the next century. The main source of urban population increase is natural increase from within the cities. However, even at only 30 per cent of the overall population, these places are of enormous importance. The pace and intensity of city life, the speed at which ideas and rumours can be transmitted in the urban environment, means that social groups can be mobilised, literally come out on to the streets, and overthrow governments (see box 3.9).

Box 3.9   *Food prices and urban riots*

In April 1985, the government of the Sudan was overthrown by massive popular demonstrations. The streets of Khartoum and other major cities were full of demonstrators. These demonstrators were from all sections of society, civil servants, teachers, day labourers, doctors. The soldiers and the police refused to fire on them. The spark which set the whole thing off was that the price of bread was raised because the government's creditors said that food subsidies had to be ended.

This was not an isolated instance. Similar demonstrations, and for very much the same reasons, have occurred in Egypt, Tunisia and Morocco in recent years. It is often the urban people who enter into direct confrontation with the government. If you live in a town, you are entirely dependent on the market for your income and for your food and shelter. Sudden rises in the price of these things, or threats to wage levels (which is the same thing), are bound to produce a sharp reaction and clear, often violent, expression of discontent.

How far can such events be seen as 'class' actions? We have seen that people in towns have many kinds of identification (see box 3.2), and class is only one of them. Within a Marxist sociology, class is seen as a relation to the means of production. People can be divided up into proletarians and bourgeoisie, employed and employers. But in the Third World, formal employment in a factory, a mine or an office is often very difficult to find. As we shall see in chapter 4, Third World cities differ from those in Europe and North America by not being based on widespread industrial development. Many people spend their lives in occasional casual employment in the service sector, working when they can as mechanics, shining shoes, washing cars, selling cigarettes, and sometimes as beggars and prostitutes. This kind of employment/unemployment is called the 'informal sector'. The idea of the informal sector is explained in box 3.10.

Box 3.10 *Formal and informal sectors in Kenya*

John Weeks studied the informal sector in Kenya in the 1970s. Although he writes as though it consists entirely of men when in fact many of the people who work in it are women supporting families, he provides a clear description.

'The basis of the formal–informal division lies in the relationship of economic activity to the state. The formal sector corresponds to what most authors call the "modern" sector, and includes both capitalist and state enterprises and institutions. Formal sector capitalist enterprise is large scale, uses capital intensive and imported techniques, and is organised on the basis of the wage labour system. The informal sector is small scale, uses labour-intensive and local or locally adapted techniques, and is organised on the basis of family labour, clientage or apprenticeship. . . . Through tariffs and quotas, the state protects producers of certain products from foreign competition. . . . The informal sector in Kenya is defined by more than . . . the absence of state favours. In many cases it is actively suppressed and discouraged. For example, the small-scale carpenter not only is limited in his ability to expand by lack of access to cheap credit, foreign exchange and technical expertise. He may also be unable to obtain a licence to operate, and works in the constant apprehension that he may be closed down by the police. If he wishes to bid for a government furniture contract, he will find that payment may be delayed months after delivery, that the standards of workmanship imposed are based on United Kingdom specifications and beyond possibility given his tools and training.'

(Weeks, J., Imbalance and the 'Employment Crisis' in Kenya, in Oxaal, I., Barnett, T., and Booth, D., *Beyond the Sociology of Development*, Routledge and Kegan Paul, 1975, p. 89.)

In some planning circles, the informal sector has been seen not as a problem, but as a possibility – a pool of entrepreneurial talent which wise policy measures should encourage so that these people can make their contribution to development. On the other hand, the concept has been criticised for being too general, as obscuring the big differences between, for example, the position of beggars and small scale artisans. It has also been noted that the mixed working found in the informal sector, people doing different work at different times of the day, week, month or year, is not restricted to towns. It is also found in rural communities (see reading 1, chapter 9). From another direction, it has been suggested that the term disguises the existence of quite ordinary class relationships, and that the informal sector is a pool of unemployed cheap labour and a few artisans (sometimes people move from one to the other and back again) which confronts the power of the large companies and the state.

This brings us back to the question of how far we can talk of classes and class action in Third World towns. I think it is difficult to generalise. Sometimes people will unite to defend their interests as a class. This may take the form of joining a trade union or joining a riot. When this will happen, and when class identity will override other ethnic or cultural affiliations, is difficult to predict. However, as we saw in the case of the food riots (box 3.9) it does happen, and is often focused on the state, which as Weeks suggests (box 3.10) often discriminates against the urban poor. The background of opinion against which such class identity can develop is described in box 3.11.

Box 3.11   *Class consciousness in Agege: Nigeria*

Adrian Peace studied a group of factory workers in Agege, an industrial suburb of Lagos. He writes:

'. . . it is scarcely surprising that . . . workers frequently articulate a marked sense of resentment against the prosperity of the few by comparison with their own relatively poverty stricken circumstances . . . it is to be expected that at times of industrial and political conflict, the manifest injustice of these gross . . .

inequalities becomes one of the major grounds on which workers justify a challenge to the authority of those in government circles. . . . Hostility towards the political order is quite as widespread amongst the self-employed who comprise the majority of townspeople in Agege. Among the factory workers' fellow townsmen, the tailors, small traders, blacksmiths, motor mechanics, drivers and carpenters, one continually encounters highly unfavourable assessments of the extreme concentration of wealth and power in the hands of a privileged minority.'

(Peace, A., *Choice, Class and Conflict*, Harvester Press, 1979, pp. 140–141.)

One important factor which may prevent the development of class identity is that Third World urbanites may retain close links with the rural areas. We saw something of this in the case of the Reds, Rascals and Gentlemen (box 3.3), where many of the men spend their lives circulating between urban employment and rural life. This circulation is maintained in South Africa through the apartheid system. But in other places, people may spend part of the year, or a few years, in town. In either case, their migration is a complex process which links town to countryside in many ways, both economic and cultural. We shall look at the rural areas in chapter 5. But first of all we must turn our attention to the vital question of industrialisation in the Third World.

4

Industrialisation

Sociology and Industrialisation

We have seen in chapter 1 that, in some respects, industrialisation is one of the original problems of sociology. It is a major concern of the sociology of development.

Many of the dichotomies, pairs of opposites, which are to be found in sociological writing attempt to describe the distinctions between industrial and pre-industrial societies. From pre-sociological writers like Henry Maine (1822–1888), through Durkheim and Tonnies, to more recent writers such as Redfield (1897–1958), Etzioni and Eisenstadt (writing in the 1960s and 1970s), the emphasis has been on the attempt to describe the distinctive features of industrial society, and sometimes the processes through which the transition comes about from pre-industrial to industrial society.

In many cases, the features which were said to describe pre-industrial society were based more on myth and belief than on research and historical scholarship. In the same way, the particular characteristics suggested as important measures of industrial, 'modern' society have been selective.

Nonetheless, one of the features said to distinguish the developed from the underdeveloped world is the existence of industry in the former and its absence in the latter. This suggests that we should be clear as to what 'industrialisation' means (see box 4.1).

Industry and Industrial Society

Box 4.1 *Industrialisation*

'The term industrialisation is meant to denote a phase in economic development in which capital and labour resources shift both relatively and absolutely from agricultural activities into industry, especially manufacturing. The rise in the factory system, increasing urbanisation, and movement from rural areas partly describes the nature of the process.'

(Industrialisation and Deindustrialisation, John Cornwall, in *The Social Science Encyclopaedia*, Kuper, A. and J., (eds.), Routledge and Kegan Paul, 1985, p. 386.)

We might add to this an important feature of industrial production, the division of labour and the discipline which this imposes on the labour process. The eighteenth century Scottish economist Adam Smith (1723–90) used the example of pin manufacture to illustrate this:

'. . . in the way in which this business is now carried on, not only the whole work is a peculiar trade, but is divided into a number of branches . . . one man draws out the wire, another straights it, a third cuts it, a fourth points it, a fifth grinds it at the top for receiving the head . . . it is even a peculiar trade by itself to put them into the paper; and the important business of making a pin is, in this manner, divided into about eighteen distinct operations. . . . Each person . . . making a tenth part of forty-eight thousand pins, might be considered as making four thousand eight hundred pins in a day. But if all had wrought separately and independently, without . . . being educated to this peculiar business, they could certainly not each of them have made twenty, perhaps not one pin in a day. . . .'

(Smith, A., *The Wealth of Nations*, Penguin, 1973, p. 110, first published 1773.)

Above all, you should note that industrialisation takes production out of the household and into the factory.

All human societies make objects for their use, and have crafts and craft specialists. But these cannot accurately be referred to as 'industrial workers', and their societies could not be called 'industrial'. On the other hand, even societies like those of western Europe, the Soviet Union and North America are not wholly industrial, having large and important agricultural sectors. Industrial production can be contrasted with craft production in terms of its scale; the employment of large numbers of workers; the use of machinery; the resulting geographical concentration; and production for a large market. Note that these features mean that some agricultural production (such as battery farming, or plantation agriculture) could be considered as industrial production.

In order to define the extent of an industrial society, we can ask what proportion of the national income is generated by industrial activities. The International Standard Industrial Classification of the United Nations provides a broad framework for deciding what sectors of a nation's productive activities can be described as 'industry' (see box 4.2).

Box 4.2 *International Standard Industrial Classification*

1. AGRICULTURE agriculture
   hunting
   forestry
   fishing

2. INDUSTRY mining, quarrying
   manufacturing
   electricity
   gas
   water
   construction

3. SERVICES wholesale and retail trade
   restaurants and hotels
   transport, storage and communications
   finance, insurance, real estate and

---

business services
community and social services.

The classification in box 4.2 is not clear-cut – and you might think, for example, whether or not the processing of agricultural products should go into the agricultural or the industrial pigeon-hole. This depends on how you define 'industrial society' (see box 4.3).

Box 4.3 *Industrial society: a definition*

For our purposes, the key features of an 'industrial' society seem to be the type of technology employed in production, the scale of organisation of labour in relation to that technology, and the extent of specialisation (or division of labour) between different parts of the production process.

The appearance of these features of industrialisation and industrial society led to more general changes in social organisation – the kinds of change that Tonnies in his distinction between *Gemeinschaft* and *Gesellschaft* and Durkheim in his distinction between organic and mechanical solidarity, were trying to capture. These writers were referring not only to technical changes, but above all to changes in the way people come to see themselves and others, changes in the ideological framework, or if you like, to use the term that Weber employed, 'the meaning of the situation'. In other words, cultural changes. Indeed, Weber's account of the relation between the development of Protestant beliefs and capitalist society points us very firmly towards a change in the attitudes and expectations of people in industrial societies.

Weber noted that capitalism requires and encourages, and works best, when the dominant belief emphasises planning, efficiency and careful accounting; in particular, when people try to account for the possible future effects of present actions.

It would be quite possible for the economy of a country such as Zambia to have a very large proportion of its national income derived from the industrial sector – according to the UN classification above – and yet not to be sociologically speaking an 'industrial' society because the majority of the population has not experienced an ideological transformation. In fact, of course, as with many sociological categories, we are really concerned with questions of degree here – the degree to which any society is characterised by the dominance of these industrial modes of productive organisation, beliefs and qualities of relationship.

Some features of industrial society are also features of urban society, although, as noted above, they are not restricted to urban society. Farming can be organised as an industry, with division of labour, large scale operation, wage workers and managers. We even have a term for this in everyday speech, when we talk about 'factory farming' (see box 4.4 for an example of agriculture organised as industry). We can also note here that the types of measure that are being used to describe 'industrial society' are not restricted to one alone, and neither do they all necessarily change in the same direction or at the same rate.

Box 4.4   *A collective farm in the Soviet Union*

Caroline Humphrey studied a collective farm in a remote central Asian region of the Soviet Union, near to Mongolia. In this extract, we can see how the administration of the farm appears to resemble that of a factory:

'The Karl Marx kolkhoz (collective farm) in Selenga district in 1967 was an "estate of production" . . . the Chairman's job is concerned with both production and administration. He is responsible for work discipline, issuing permits for travel, sick-leave, insurance and pensions, taking on and dismissing workers, and the honesty and quality of their work, as well as the directly productive activities of allotting products and money to different funds, obtaining inputs, fulfilling the plan of delivery

> to the state, allocating machinery and workers to the brigades, and so on.'
>
> (Humphrey, C., *Karl Marx Collective*, Cambridge University Press and Editions de la Maison des Sciences de l'Homme, Cambridge and Paris, 1983, pp. 119–122.)

Industry and Rationality

Like everybody else, peasant farmers make rational decisions and plan for the future most of the time – they have to or they do not survive – but they do not produce on a large scale using lots of labour and advanced methods; captains of industry can bet on irrational hunches as well as read computer printouts of market projections; farming can take the form of extremely sophisticated computer controlled irrigation combined with chemical pest control. In an industrial society, all the broad features – large scale organisation, specialisation, the dominance of rational calculation in relation to various markets (for labour, capital, land, products) – all come together to affect the entire society. How this happens, the process of industrialisation, is the subject of the next section.

The Industrialisation Process

There are broadly two different ways of analysing the origins of industrialisation. Marxists identify the origin of industry with the development of capitalism. This view assumes that as technical progress occurs it allows for greater production and potentially improved welfare for members of society. However, the existing relations of production, the forms in which property is held, the taken-for-granted beliefs about how much of the total product should go to different groups in the production process, the view of who contributes what value to production, all these things act as fetters to the realisation of the productive potential of a society. A *contradiction* is said to exist between the forces (technology, technical knowledge, crafts) of production, and the relations (legal arrangements, social organisation, forms of contract, forms of distribution, beliefs about the correct organisation of society) of production. This contradiction appears in various forms, ranging from local riots, withdrawal of labour, to protest of a cultural kind. But in its most pronounced form, the social groups or classes which are most exploited by the prevailing system organise to overthrow the dominant group or class.

This is not only a view of the origins of industry and of capitalism, it is a general theory about how social change and development takes place. It can be used to talk about the transition from pre-industrial and pre-capitalist societies to capitalist industrial society as well as to later projected stages of development, in particular the transition to a socialist society. Most of Marx's analysis was concerned with understanding how capitalist society worked – remember that his main work is called *Das Kapital*. Much of the recent work of Marxist scholars who are interested in the Third World has been concerned with the question of how the transition to industrial capitalist society can or might take place. This problem was central to the work of Frank and Warren outlined in chapter 2.

The other main tradition has its origins in Durkheim's sociology, and emphasises the growing interdependence arising from the division of labour in society. As you might expect, it has tended to contain functionalist assumptions, and to emphasise the ways in which industrialisation gives rise to problems of functional interdependence and a tendency for social disorder – social pathology of one kind or another – to appear with the spread of industrial production.

From within this perspective, industrialisation is seen to flow from attempts to solve problems arising from increased population density, which Durkheim thought a major cause of the division of labour. This approach also stresses the role of ideas and of the inventions – both technical and social – which arise from new ideas. In many respects, modernisation theories are firmly in this category. The key problem of industrialisation in this view, is not the process itself, but rather the social problems which arise from it. Thus 'anomie' is a major problem, both at the level of the individual and also the whole society. This Durkheimian view manifests itself in modernisation theory and its concern with social 'integration' and 'malintegration'. We can see this in their discussion of urbanisation and politics (see box 4.5).

Box 4.5   *The integration of society*

C. E. Black, writing about the politics of modernisation in the 1960s, chose the term 'integrated society' as most aptly describing a society which had successfully modernised:

'The essence of this phase . . . (in development) . . . is that the great movement of peoples from the countryside to the city transforms the structure of society from one of relatively autonomous regional, organisational, and occupational groupings to one that is highly fragmented and in which the individual is relatively isolated.

The concept of integration . . . means in particular that the individual's ties with local, regional, and other immediate structures are reduced at the same time that his ties with the larger and more diffuse urban and industrial networks are strengthened . . . a society that reaches this stage of integration can make much more use of its human resources . . . the more highly a society is mechanised, the more susceptible it is to paralysing forms of disorganisation. In times of disorder . . . it is plagued by the possibility of large-scale unemployment and social unrest. In less integrated societies there is also extensive unemployment, or perhaps more accurately underemployment.'

(Black, C. E., *The Dynamics of Modernisation*, Harper and Row, New York and London, 1966, pp. 67–68.)

Within this general theory, industrialisation is seen as a key component of modernisation. The role of the entrepreneurial individual is emphasised, although this is not meant only to include industrial entrepreneurs, but inventive individuals in general.

McClelland's idea of the need for achievement, 'Nach' (see box 4.6), crystallises this view of the motive force in social change in general and the industrialisation process as a particular case of social change.

Box 4.6 *Need for achievement*

Writing in 1961, McClelland said:

'My . . . concern is not with all culture growth, but with economic growth. . . . I am interested in the internal factors – in the values and motives men have that lead them to exploit opportunities, to take advantage of favorable trade conditions; in short, to shape their own destiny. . . . Chief among these motives was what we termed "the need for Achievement" (*n* Achievement) – a desire to do well, not so much for the sake of social recognition or prestige, but to attain an inner feeling of personal accomplishment.'

(McClelland, D., The Achievement Motive in Economic Growth, in Hoselitz, B. F., and Moore, W. E. (eds.) *Industrialisation and Society*, 1966, pp. 74–76.)

Wilbert E. Moore (*Social Change*, Prentice Hall, New York, 1964) sums up the general conditions which bring about society-wide industrialisation (see box 4.7).

Box 4.7 *Moore and the conditions for industrialisation*

The general conditions for industrialisation:

1. Change in values: this is fundamental, and involves adoption of rational ways of solving problems, combined with a nationalistic basis of identity which is supposed to cater for the non-rational needs of people; in particular it is the basis upon which society-wide mobilisation can be built.

---

2. Change in institutions: the requisite changes here are predominantly to do with the development of market relations in labour and in property. Other types of arrangement – such as collectively held property and unpaid labour organised on, for example, kinship lines – are seen as obstacles to be overcome in the transition to industrial society.

3. Changes in organisations: meaning the introduction of hierarchically administered government and civil service, as well as in the individual enterprise.

4. Change in motivation: as Moore puts it, 'a simple desire for a better life' which is to be combined with the spread of participation so that people can feel that they are involved in and affecting change.

McClelland and others conclude from this that Nach can be learned, and that development can be achieved through a process of 'diffusion' of culture, ideas and technology.

There are many problems with this model of industrialisation. In particular, it tends to look at existing industrial societies and assume that their characteristics are those necessary to bring about industrialisation in the future in other places – that the effect of a process can be the cause of the same process in another place. No adequate account of how they came to have these features is provided by these theorists. The following comment by Moore sums up the problem:

How these changes are to be brought about in developing areas now must probably be given a different answer from that provided by their often slow development in the history of the industrialised Western World. Although no single instigating agency of deliberate change is likely to be absolutely sovereign, even in a totalitarian society, the state is likely to be more influential than any other social structure in a pluralistic society.

(Moore, W. E., 1964, p. 97.)

You might ask yourself some questions about this view; for example:

1. How 'slow' were the changes in the presently industrialised countries?

2. How far were the changes which brought about industrialisation purely internal?

3. What 'external' factors might be taken into account?

4. Is there only one 'history' of industrialisation, or are there disagreements about this 'history'?

The economic historian Alexander Gerschenkron, in his book *Economic Backwardness in Historical Perspective* (Harvard University Press, Cambridge, Mass., 1962), emphasised that the development of the late developers could be both helped and hindered by the experience of those societies which were already developed. The rules of the game were changed by the impact of each successive development experience.

Weber and Industrialisation

Two other sociological theories of industrialisation are of importance. One is that proposed by Max Weber, the other is known as the convergence thesis.

I noted earlier that Weber's book *The Protestant Ethic and the Spirit of Capitalism* is really only a part of a much bigger study, the aim of which was to test the relation between economic change and religious beliefs. He argues that people's economic activities are influenced by their religious beliefs. Weber suggests that the development of capitalism as the general form of economic organisation in certain north European countries resulted, at least in part, from the adoption of Calvinist Christianity by some merchants and craftworkers. The beliefs of Calvinism emphasise individual responsibility, hard work, plain living, saving and planning for the future. These qualities were just the right ones for the development of capitalism, but they did not *cause* it. Rather, they fitted with the economic and social conditions which already existed, but provided an added impetus in the direction of capitalism. It is important not to misunderstand Weber – he was not saying that Calvinism caused capitalism. He was saying that it gave it a very strong push forward; indeed, in some other parts of the world, like China, Weber says, the social and economic conditions were very similar to those in Europe, but there were no beliefs equivalent to Calvinism to help them along.

Much research has been done to test this hypothesis. Notable is Robert Bellah's book *Tokugawa Religion: the values of pre-industrial Japan* (Glencoe, Illinois, 1957), which argues that the ascetic, disciplined culture of the aristocratic Samurai warriors enabled them to become the basis of Japan's impressive capitalist industrialisation. In a different, rural, context Parkin's study of the Giriama people of Kenya (Parkin, D. J., *Palms, Wine and Witnesses*, Intertext Books, 1972) and Long's study of the Lala people of Zambia (Long, N., *Social Change and the Individual: a study of the social and religious responses to innovation*, Manchester University Press, 1968), both suggest that people who are in a position to become innovators and entrepreneurs may adopt a new religious belief, in part because this gives them access to mutual aid from other believers, in part because it allows them to get out of traditional obligations which might drain their capital away (see box 4.8).

Box 4.8   *Islamisation among the Giriama*

The Giriama people used to keep cattle and practise subsistence cultivation. Rights to land, and to the produce of particular trees, were protected by elders of the society, who bore witness to ownership in case of dispute. During the 1920s and 1930s, they began to cultivate coconut trees for the cash crop, copra. Some of them began to accumulate wealth from this. These people were faced with a problem:

'On the one hand, they must subscribe to the common language of custom as a means of placing and controlling investment (remember that ownership has to be witnessed by the elders). On the other, their long-term aims are to expand and diversify their economic enterprises and reduce their dependence on farming. . . .'

These people were often criticised for not keeping to expensive customs such as funeral and marriage payments, involving feasting and drinking palm wine:

'There operates in this event what we might call the principle of ritual distinctiveness. A number of successful farmers and entrepreneurs who are subject to intense pressures . . . undergo possession by a so-called Islamic spirit. After diagnosis by a diviner . . . they are obliged 'to become Muslim', to the extent only of observing the fast of Ramadhan and the Islamic prohibition on alcohol and the meat of animals which have not been slaughtered by Muslims. Palm-wine is drunk daily by Giriama and collective meat-eating ceremonies are frequent and intense. A consequence of this release from close commensal relations is that it signifies and categorises the relationships between a successful farmer and his ordinary neighbours and friends. . . .'

(Parkin, D. J., 1972, pp. 2–3.)

Such Weberian theory is not directly concerned with industrialisation. It is about entrepreneurship and inventiveness and its place in social and historical change. These things do happen without industrialisation resulting, all societies have their inventors. But as the theory of entrepreneurship claims to be a partial explanation of the origins of capitalism, and industrial production is central to capitalism, then the theory also claims to explain the origins of industrialisation.

Convergence Theory

Another set of theories which comment on industrialisation is known as the convergence thesis. This is found in the work of Clark Kerr (Kerr, C., Dunlop, J. and Harbin, F., *Industrialism and Industrial Man*, Heinemann, 1960). They argue that industrial production requires:

1. high cost investment – leading to a spread of power among a lot of different people, technical specialists and administrators;

2. decentralisation – dependence on many and diverse specialists means that power is diffused to many different groups in society;

3. meritocratic selection – dependence on technical expertise means that the most appropriate and the best people have to be given power and authority, rather than those who 'inherit' power, either through their families or some other form of succession.

They conclude that poverty disappears because workers organise to get higher wages, heavy manual labour is no longer in demand and people move into more technical and service types of employment. The modern state assumes greater responsibility for welfare. They consider that state socialism, as in the USSR, is just another way of legitimating attempts at industrialisation. In the end, all industrial societies will exhibit similar characteristics, and will end up looking rather like western Europe or North America.

This view of industrialisation seems to place most of the weight of explanation on the ways in which the technology of production determines the forms of social, economic and political organisation. One prediction of this theory was that the socialist countries with their planned economies, and the capitalist economies with their emphasis on the free market, would increasingly converge, leading to an 'end of ideology', which was the title of a book by one member of this school, Daniel Bell. Long considered an inadequate theory because of its technological determinism, recent changes in China and the Soviet Union might make us give it some serious consideration. Although it is certainly not an adequate theory of how industrialisation can be brought about, it may be a useful description of features common to industrial societies in general. And it is certainly true that some parts of the Third World are becoming industrial societies, notably in East Asia, where Taiwan, Singapore, South Korea and Hong Kong have experienced radical transformation in the last twenty years.

The Conditions for Industrialisation

Critics of modernisation theory made it clear that industrialisation in the Third World was unlikely to follow the same pattern as in the developed world. Latecomers enter a different game in which the rules have been changed. In this section we look at some of these rules, and see how industrialisation has occurred, and what form it has taken. Consideration of this problem has its roots in the trauma of the Second World War, when many Third World countries were cut off from the industrial heartlands of Europe and North America (see box 4.9).

Box 4.9 *Isolation and industrialisation*

'As new nation-states arose to form the so-called Third World, so the demand for industrial development grew in these countries. During the Second World War, when competition from the developed countries had been blunted by shipping blockades and the like, a small industrial bourgeoisie had arisen in some of the less developed countries. Some of these manufacturers as well as traders and merchants in the richer of the Third World Countries looked to the manufacturing sector for continued capital accumulation. And politicians in the newly independent countries were looking at industrialisation as a path to development not only for the countries, but also for themselves. Some at least of the politically powerful saw a potential for their own material gain in the development of locally based industrial companies in which directorships might become available.'

(Edwards, C. B., *The Fragmented World*, Methuen, London and New York, 1985, p. 211.)

In this extract you should note that industrialisation is said to have its roots in the interests of classes. It is not the result of some 'natural' process of growth.

 This isolation led to the idea of 'import substituting industrialisation'. Many people, especially in Latin America, were concerned that the Third World could not continue, as it had in the colonial period, to be a source mainly of primary products (minerals and agricultural) which were produced in the Third World but processed in the developed world. Not only was there a limited demand for these products, but their prices were falling relative to the prices of manufactured products. In other words, there were 'adverse terms of trade', you had to produce more and more primary products to buy the same amount of imported manufactured goods. Primary production was unlikely to lead to economic growth for other reasons too (see box 4.9).

Box 4.9 *Primary production, 'linkages' and 'infant industries'*

'. . . by the 1960s there was considerable pessimism about the revenue-generating potential of primary products . . . (some). . . . Economists also argued that the primary sector was inherently backward compared to the manufacturing sector, because of the latter's *linkages* (both within the sector and between the manufacturing industries and other parts of the economy), and because of the allegedly greater *economies of scale* in manufacturing. . . . Thus once a manufacturing industry was established, it was much more likely to attract other activities around it, because of its demands both on supplies from other industries and on a supporting infrastructure, as well as through its turnover of a skilled and disciplined labour force . . . the promotion of industrialisation by government intervention found both "material" support [see box 4.8] in the less developed countries and theoretical justification. It was argued that this promotion would have to come from *protection* – from reserving domestic markets for these newly founded industries . . . these were *infant industries*, which needed a period of

> nurturing away from the cold winds of world competition. . . .
> And so the infant industry argument was used to justify the
> protection which developed in the Third World in the 1960s.'
>
> (Edwards, C. B., 1985, pp. 211–212.)

Export substituting industrialisation did not work.
Although during the 1960s industrial exports from the Third
World grew rapidly from about $3 billion in 1960 to more than
$9 billion in 1970, and had reached $80 billion by 1980 (C.
Edwards, 1985, p. 218), this was not the result of import substi-
tution. It was the result of what has been called the 'New
International Division of Labour'.

Import substitution ran into the following problems:

1. From box 4.10, you will see that the 'infant industries' had
to be protected by government policies – tariffs, import quotas,
artificially low prices for raw materials. This meant that industrialists, protected from the market, could not make 'rational'
decisions about what and how much to produce.

2. New industries needed machinery and technical know-how.
These had to be imported. Imports required foreign currency.
Foreign currency could only be earned by increasing exports of
primary products.

3. Machinery and know-how could be obtained from large
international companies, known as TNCs (Trans National
Corporations). Such companies would only invest if it was in
their interests, and they were not going to invest without wanting
to sell in the local market, thus undermining the 'infant
industries'.

4. There was limited demand for industrial goods in the Third
World, because most people were too poor to buy them. They
might want televisions, cars, soft drinks and other luxury goods,
but first they wanted decent housing, food and shelter.

The failure of import substituting industrialisation meant that
a new approach had to be tried (see box 4.10). It was this that

largely led to the rapid growth of manufactured exports in the 1970s and early 1980s which was referred to above. This new approach has been called 'export oriented industrialisation'.

Box 4.10   *Dependency theory and the failure of import substituting industrialisation*

Dependency theory has its roots in the failure of import substituting industrialisation in Latin America:

'The theory of dependency is the response to the perceived failure of national development through import substitution industrialisation ... by the 1960s ... it had become obvious ... that ... import substitution had not lessened dependence. Income substitution seemed to be growing more unequal, and a large segment of the population remained marginal. Cultural alienation was widespread, and Latin American societies still continued divided and unstable. National policies for industrialisation had succumbed to the multi-national corporations, and industrialisation in Latin America was primarily being undertaken by foreign investors.... The theory of dependence emerged as an attempt to explain this failure.'

(O'Brien, P., A Critique of Latin American Theories of Dependency, in Oxaal, I., et. al. (eds.), 1975, pp. 10–11.)

It is this kind of industrialisation which has been tried in East Asia and in Brazil, and not without success. In the early 1970s, South Korea's exports grew at a rate of more than 20 per cent per year (Edwards, C. B., 1985, p. 296). Most of this industrialisation has been based on light industry (although South Korea has a large steel, shipbuilding and motor car sector), like electronics and clothing. This development has been based on massive state intervention and on all kinds of special conditions which, it could be argued, cannot be replicated in other countries (see box 4.11). We should also note that in most of these countries, there is a high level of ethnic and cultural unity which has perhaps, under the guise of nationalism, allowed very repressive political regimes to push through harsh policies of low wages and long working hours. This nationalism, which must be contrasted with the ethnic, religious and cultural differentiation in India and much of Africa, has been reinforced by proximity to Communist China and its perceived threat to societies with large populations who are refugees from communism, as in Taiwan and Hong Kong.

Box 4.11   *Special factors and political repression in the 'Four Little Tigers'*

'. . . the major factor in Hong Kong's success can be . . . argued to be its special relationship with the Chinese hinterland, from which it has received a massive inflow of not only immigrant labour, but also capital. . . . In the case of South Korea . . . there is substantial evidence of massive state intervention to promote industrial growth . . . subsidies from the state and profitable trade arising from the war in Vietnam, played significant roles in both South Korea and Taiwan. . . . In Singapore these factors were less important, but nevertheless played some part.'

(Edwards, C. B., 1985, p. 296.)

'Many governments do rely predominantly on force. The military hardware trundled out on Independence Day to impress the citizenry is light equipment designed for counter-insurgency – for class war against their own people, not some foreign enemy. . . . East Asian countries . . . "have endured unprecedently long reigns of unbroken repression against popular organisations of any kind: 140 years in the case of Hong Kong: nearly a century in Taiwan and South Korea. Nowhere in the world, except South Africa, can compare with this record".'

(Worsley, P. M., *The Three Worlds*, Weidenfield and Nicholson, 1986, p. 228.)

We do not know whether or not the experience of these

countries can be repeated in other places. There is a view which says that it is unlikely. This comes from world system theory, and points to the role of the transnational corporations. While writing this book, my word-processor broke and I had to look inside it. On the circuit board, I found a variety of components, each with its country of origin printed on it. They came from Taiwan, Singapore, Hong Kong, El Salvador and Mexico. So the parts of my word-processor had travelled thousands of miles before they were assembled. This is one symptom of what is sometimes called the *decomposition of capital*, the process whereby large companies are able to spread the different stages of production between different countries, depending on where they can get the best deal in terms of low wages, high skills and government support. Such support often takes the form of Export Processing Zones. These are special areas within a country where foreign investors are provided with very favourable conditions, such as tax-holidays and waivers on import duties. Such zones are also found in Britain, and there have been cases where large transnational corporations set up a business, stay as long as they can reap the special benefits, and leave after a few years when somewhere else becomes more attractive.

In this view, the world system can be seen as capitalism writ large – transnationals controlling capital, and an international, and nationally divided, proletariat (often the very cheapest and most oppressed labour force is women) doing the work. The advance which this view makes over dependency theory is that it allows that a certain type of development can occur, in countries of the 'semi-periphery', which, like Brazil and the Four Little Tigers, are situated midway between the metropolis and satellites of the dependency model.

The Call for a New International Economic Order (NIEO)

Despite rapid and impressive industrialisation in some parts of the Third World, most countries still depend heavily on primary production. With the major part of their population in agricultural production, they are understandably concerned to obtain the best possible prices for their cash crops. You will recall that earlier I talked about the problem of the terms of trade between primary and manufactured products.

In the early 1970s, many Third World countries called for the establishment of a NIEO. The idea was to form a kind of 'trade union of the Third World'. One outcome of this was the formation of the 'Group of 77', which in fact now has more than 120 members. This was not very effective, in part because primary producers end up competing with each other to sell their products, and trade unions only work if the members work in unison. One organisation which has been quite successful until recently is the Organization of Petroleum Exporting Countries (OPEC). But the future for concerted action by exporters of agricultural products does not look very optimistic. World markets are, after all, markets. They do not take account of social needs in the Third World. Despite calls by the Brandt Commission (Brandt, W., *North–South: A Programme for Survival*, Pan Books, 1983) for fairer relations between the rich 'north' and the poor 'south' because of some assumed common interest, profit seems to be more important than 'fairness'.

Summary

We have seen that the problem of industrialisation is one of the key problems of sociology in general, and a major concern of the sociology of development. Industrialisation takes production out of the home and the household into the wider world.

Modernisation theory, building on the ideas of Durkheim and Weber, emphasises that industrialisation involves changes in people's attitudes and expectations as well as in the structure of their relationships. Weber, discussing rationalisation, noted that capitalism requires cultural changes, emphasising planning, efficiency, and careful accounting. We have seen the close connection between urbanisation and industrialisation, although we must not forget that farming can be industrialised, and that peasants are as rational as industrialists.

I made it clear that there are two different ways of analysing the origins of industrialisation. Marxists identify the origin of industry with the development of capitalism, although there are serious disagreements within this tradition, exemplified in the theories of Frank and Warren. The Durkheimians emphasise the growing interdependence arising from the division of labour in society.

Alexander Gerschenkron cautioned against projecting the future from the experience of past industrialisation, because each experience changes the rules for those that come later.

I also emphasised that the Weberian contribution concentrates on the place of entrepreneurship, and noted that perhaps convergence theory needed to be given more serious attention.

We looked at how import substitution policies had failed, and in their failure gave rise to dependency theory, and a move to export led industrialisation, with its special conditions which seem to have enabled the Four Little Tigers and some other countries to industrialise. What this theory seems to show is the development of an international working class as a result of the activities of transnational corporations. Important in this development has been state intervention, through subsidies to investment and the imposition of political conditions in which the labour force is disciplined and prevented from organising to protect its own interests.

In this chapter I have mentioned that 'the state' has an important part to play in development. I shall have more to say about this in chapter 7.

5

Rural development: entering the market

So far, we have looked at problems of urbanisation and industrialisation. But, in most countries of the Third World, the typical way of life is rural and most probably agricultural – families and households working together to produce crops and animals either to support themselves or to sell for cash, or more likely a mixture of these activities.

A very important problem for the sociology of development is how the transition occurs from subsistence production and subsistence society, to production for the market and involvement in a much larger set of social and economic relationships. This process is called 'agrarian and rural change'. As with industrialisation, it is central to all sociology. It is, after all, the opposite side of the same coin. In Western societies, the change occurred nearly two hundred years ago (see box 1.3). Of course, recalling the 'Gerschenkron thesis', we should not expect it to follow the same pattern. The past is rarely a good predictor of the future in social matters. However, agrarian and rural change is of central importance in the Third World today. And in both the Soviet Union and China it presented, and continues to present, many difficulties.

Some False Impressions of the Third World

Most of us have some vague impression of how people in other societies live. For example, it is often assumed that in Africa and the Pacific, people live in 'tribes', while in India, the 'caste system' is important. Many of these images are inaccurate – they often reflect the very poor understanding of these social systems which was propagated during the colonial period, but which still hangs on in the way that we are taught history or geography. For example, in Africa, people do often have very strong allegiances to groups other than the nation, but these are not necessarily what you may think of as a 'tribe' (see box 3.2 in which the complexity of people's attachments is explored). You may believe that a 'tribe' is an hierarchical organisation with a 'chief' who tells everybody what to do. In fact, there are many different forms of social organisation in Africa. Some people, like the Nuer, a pastoral people in the Southern Sudan, live in very small groups for much of the year, have no leaders, and very little sense of identity as 'Nuer'. On a day-to-day basis, they are much more likely to identify with their household or the group of households with whom they live and work. At the other end of the spectrum, there are people whose social organisation is hierarchical and do have leaders. The Hausa people of northern Nigeria would to some extent fit this picture.

Until the advent of colonialism, there were many different social and economic arrangements in Africa and the Pacific. The Nuer led lives which were quite isolated from other people around them (although they were raided for slaves throughout the nineteenth century by the Arabs). The Hausa, in contrast, had trading and political relationships with many other societies, and in particular with the world of Islam to the north.

In Africa prior to colonisation, then, one could have found both great, centralised states and small, localised and fragmented societies, together with many intermediate types. In Asia, larger political units were the norm. But even so, their degree of control over rural society would vary. In the Pacific, small scale organisation was the norm, but even here, in Hawaii, larger states did sometimes exist. These cultures, and here we should emphasise the *cultural* component, form the basis of the present-day states, most of which were established by colonial governments. Notable exceptions to this pattern are Ethiopia and Thailand, although even these did not remain unaffected by the colonial impact.

Colonialism and Capitalism: from 'Savage' to 'Peasant'

A central problem for us is to understand how pre-capitalist, subsistence societies became part of the world system. To understand this, we need to know something of why the colonial expansion took place. There are different views about this. A common one is that Europeans set out to colonise the world as part of a 'civilising mission'. Sociologists would not dispute that this was one of the reasons the colonisers gave to explain their actions. But they would then ask why it happened when it did, and what other reasons there were. They would ask why this moral mission became so important to Europeans in the nineteenth century. Was it because of the economic and social conditions in the colonising society? They would then point to four aspects of the imperial expansion which require more detailed examination. These are:

1. the need to find markets for the products of European industrial development;

2. the demand for tropical products such as palm oil and cotton as inputs to the manufacture of cheap soap, margarine and textiles for an expanding home market as workers moved into growing towns at home;

3. the related need for cheap labour in the colonies in order to produce these tropical products;

4. strategic territory-grabbing by European powers who were in competition with each other for the resources of the Third World.

So, beneath the explicit 'civilising influence' lay very definite economic interests. How the four factors actually affected any particular act of colonisation was specific to each case. But in each case, it was important that the colonies contributed to their own colonial government by producing crops or minerals for sale on a world market (see box 5.1).

Box 5.1 *Cotton in the Sudan*

The Gezira Scheme in the Sudan is an enormous irrigated cotton plantation. It was established by the British in 1925. The reasons were as follows:

'The Sudan was of utmost importance to the strategy of the British Empire. It formed an important link in the vision of a stretch of red on the map from the Cape to Cairo. Most importantly, it was an area . . . essential to safeguarding the Suez Canal and the route to India. . . . Faced with the necessity of administering a country as undeveloped as the Sudan . . . it was essential that the British government should not be burdened by the expense . . . the answer was to try and enable the Sudan to finance its own administration. This could be done by cotton cultivation.'

(Barnett, T., *The Gezira Scheme: an illusion of development*, Frank Cass, 1977, p. 4.)

This need to produce in a new way and on a large scale for a market gave rise to a problem. Local people were frequently quite reluctant to be 'civilised', to produce for sale, or to work on plantations or in mines. There were many cases of fierce opposition to colonisation: the Ashanti people of Ghana waged a major war against the British as did the Zulu in South Africa. Apart from these and other spectacular manifestations of opposition, there were many others which were more subtle – like refusing to work. Colonial governments' response to this was to force people to go to work by imposing taxes on them – taxes which could only be paid in cash, and this cash could only be earned by going to work as a labour migrant (as in south and central Africa) or by growing crops which could be sold for cash, like palm trees for palm oil or indigo plants which form the basis of blue dyes which were in demand in the textile industries (see box 5.2).

Box 5.2   *Forced labour and taxation in West Africa*

'On the eve of the Second World War, the peasants of French West Africa had to furnish each year . . . 175,000,000 francs in poll-tax and cattle-tax, 21,000,000 days of statute labour and 12,000 soldiers. . . . To the taxes were added supplementary payments . . . levied by the chiefs; debts paid to the provident societies . . . "presents" to employees at the processing plants; commodities "requisitioned" for the entertainment of administrators . . . sales of compulsory crops below cost price. . . . Days of statute labour represented only a fraction of forced labour, excluding extra labour for the chiefs and recruitment for big public works.'

(Suret-Canale, J., The Economic Balance Sheet of French Colonialism in West Africa, in Gutkind, C. W. and Waterman, P., *African Social Studies*, Heinemann, 1977, p. 128.)

Thus, the colonial interlude was the beginning of a process whereby new relations of production and new social categories were being established. With the spread of cash-cropping, a process of **'peasantisation'** occurred, and in this process the exotic subsistence producing 'savages' of nineteenth century and early twentieth century sociology and anthropology gradually became transformed into 'peasants' and 'workers'. But while this was happening, sociological theory had a lot of catching up to do. It had to get away from the idea of Third World people as exotic 'savages', and to replace this view with another more in keeping with the realities of capitalist development. One long detour in this theoretical development involved the growing recognition that, despite different cultures, the inhabitants of the rural Third World were all becoming participants in a world market for agricultural commodities and labour.

The Market – Our Way and Their Way

One way in which we can begin to understand the process of change from subsistence production to market production is to think about a very basic but rather difficult sociological idea – that the way we live and organise our own society is neither the only nor the 'best' possible way. It is merely one form of society developed by the peoples of north western Europe. Central to these social and economic arrangements is the 'market'.

The word 'market' does not describe a place. Social scientists use the word to refer to a particular way of distributing goods and services in a society. It includes the general idea of buying and selling. This means there have to be things which can be bought and sold, and there must be a 'need' to buy and sell, in other words some division of labour, because people have specialised. Once there is a division of labour, then exchange can take place through the market. But you should note that in other societies distribution can be done through other social mechanisms, for example by ceremonial or moral means. I will talk about these ideas in some more detail later on in this chapter.

Essential to a market form of distribution are the ideas of price, competition and profit. A market requires some idea of getting the 'best' price for any particular item or 'commodity' that we value, whether that is an object or our own labour. To some extent, price will reflect the balance of supply and demand. Economists often describe this process of buyers and sellers arriving at a price as individuals expressing their 'subjective preference' – which means expressing their wants and desires for objects or services through a bidding procedure in a market.

Now, although these ideas are so familiar to most of us as to seem 'natural', it is important to realise that they are neither 'natural' nor have they always been the typical arrangement of social and economic life even in western Europe. Indeed, if you think about it, all transactions do not take this form in western Europe and North America today. The degree to which they should do is a matter of active and continuing political debate. For example, in Britain the Conservative Party is very keen on the market, while the Labour Party believes that some things, like health and education, should be equally available to everyone, and not dependent on ability to pay.

An example of a non-market transaction is blood donation. In the United Kingdom, people give and receive blood and there is no question of payment to the donor or by the recipient. For some of us, the idea of a market in blood or transplant organs may seem odd or even repugnant. In many countries, though, blood and organs are traded like any other commodity – such a trade exists on a world scale. There is no reason why they should not be, except that within the UK a political and ethical decision has been taken that transactions in this sphere should remain outside the market.

In other societies, in the past and in the present, many other areas of life have remained outside the sphere of market exchange. In fact, whereas in capitalist society most exchanges take place in the market, in other societies the reverse is the case, and most, and sometimes all, exchanges have been in the non-market sphere. In these cases, the basis upon which exchanges are made may be said to be 'moral' rather than 'economic', a point which interested Durkheim when he talked about the power of moral rules over people's behaviour. Similarly, Max Weber in his discussion of the development of the Protestant Ethic contrasted 'rational', market type relations and what he called 'non-rational', non-market, relations.

Put simply, the history and sociology (as well as the economics) of most rural parts of the Third World over the last 150 years can be seen as a progressive destruction of non-market relations and their replacement by the market. However, having said this, we must also bear in mind that it is a simplification, because even in 'developed' capitalist societies, many non-market relationships of production and consumption endure (women's work in the home being one, done for 'moral' reasons).

Market Exchange, Non-Market Exchange and Rural Change

In order to understand the sociology of change in rural societies, we have to be aware of the possibility of all kinds of mixed and transitional production and exchange relations existing side by side. For example, people may work together on some tasks without payment, because the community has a 'duty' to do that work together. In the same community, people will haggle with each other over small amounts of money for work, because that kind of work (on a cash crop for example) is considered to be in the market domain (see box 5.3).

Box 5.3 *Market and non-market relations*

An area in which market and non-market elements are often unclear is household work. As I indicated in chapter 2, peasant producers often use household labour without placing a market value upon it – they simply work until they have 'enough' ('enough' differs from society to society). The precise mixture of market and non-market exchanges, household and paid labour, in production and consumption which has developed in any case will depend on the way a society has become linked into the world system.

In Darfur, in the western Sudan, the Fur people make a clear distinction between non-market work (done by work parties in exchange for the provision of beer and food) and market transactions (the purchase and sale of items like sugar and cash crops). There are strict moral rules which separate the two spheres. Sometimes an outsider can take advantage of this division, as the following case shows.

'. . . in 1961 . . . an Arab merchant who regularly visited the market places on the northern fringes of the Marra mountains, asked for permission to spend the rainy season in a village, and asked for an area of land on which to cultivate a tomato crop. He brought his wife and settled her in a hut, and he bought a large amount of millet in the lowlands . . . where the price is very low. . . . From the millet, his wife made beer. This beer was used to call work parties, applying the labour to tomato cultivation. Without any significant labour input of his own, he thus produced a large tomato crop, which he dried and transported to El Fasher for sale. . . . On an investment of £5 worth of millet, he obtained a return of more than £100 for his tomatoes.'

(Barth, F., Economic Spheres in Darfur, in Firth, R. (ed.), *Themes in Economic Anthropology*, Tavistock, 1970, p. 171.)

This example shows how a non-market system can become linked into the wider system by the activities of an entrepreneur (literally a go-between) who spans the two spheres of exchange.

Two Schools of Thought About the Link

For many years there were two competing theories which tried to explain the similarities and differences between non-market and market societies. From these theories, it seemed that the way to link the two types was through processes of education and 'technical change'. This was because, in their different ways, both theories retained a more or less explicit notion of the exotic 'savage'.

The two sides of the argument were known as 'substantivism' and 'formalism'.

Substantivism

For the substantivists, the explanation of the different ways in which people organised their production and distribution lay in their moral beliefs. Peasants and nomads, it was said, organised their production in accordance with their traditions. In contrast, in the 'developed' world, such decisions were the outcome of rational calculation. You will recall here the emphasis that Durkheim placed on the role of moral beliefs and values in human society. And this school of thought certainly had its roots in Durkheimian sociology, believing that distribution and consumption in non-European societies was organised in response to moral imperatives. The following extract gives you some idea of how this school looked at the problem:

... there are two possible courses to affluence. Wants may be 'easily satisfied' either by producing much or desiring little. The familiar conception ... makes assumptions peculiarly appropriate to market economies: that man's wants are great, not to say infinite, whereas his means are limited, although improvable: thus the gap between means and ends can be narrowed by industrial productivity, at least to the point that 'urgent goods' become plentiful. But there is also a Zen road to affluence, departing from premises somewhat different from our own: that human material wants are finite and few, and technical means unchanging but on the whole adequate. Adopting the Zen strategy, a people can enjoy an unparalleled material plenty – with a low standard of living.

(Sahlins, M., *Stone Age Economics*, Tavistock Publications, 1974, p. 2.)

Box 5.4 *Some links*

You might like to look at this extract again later on, when you are reading about the difficulties of defining development in chapter 9, because what Sahlins calls 'the Zen strategy' is very like many of the ideas of the 'green' movement.

From this you will see that what is important is how much people decide they want to produce – in other words, what value they place upon 'infinite wants'. In this view, 'plenty' and 'enough' are relative notions, differing in different societies according to the values of those societies.

In practice this means that the rules governing what shall be produced, how much, who will do what work, who will receive how much of the product, are said to be the outcome of 'tradition'. They are not the outcome of profit-oriented decisions taken in a marketplace. It is argued that such societies 'ruled by tradition' are unlikely to be innovative, and are likely to be isolated and unchanging. Now, although the rates at which different societies change does vary, and some societies (for example in the Highlands of Papua New Guinea and in the Amazon Basin) were until relatively recently quite isolated, many of these conclusions owe more to the assumptions of the anthropologists who studied them than to fact. We can take the example of a celebrated anthropological study to illustrate this point.

In the early years of this century, Bronislav Malinowski (1884–1942) studied and then wrote about the Trobriand Islanders of New Guinea. He presented a picture of them as an isolated and self-contained society. But he was selective in his observations. He argued that they suppressed their 'natural' acquisitiveness and gave more heed to their moral rules:

[The Trobriander] . . . 'is not guided primarily by the desire to satisfy his wants, but by a very complex set of traditional forces, duties and obligations, beliefs in magic, social ambitions and vanities. He wants, if he is a man, to achieve social distinction as a 'good gardener' and a good worker in general.'

(Malinowski, B., *Argonauts of the Western Pacific*, Routledge and Kegan Paul, 1961 [first published 1922], p. 62.)

What he failed to tell his readers in the main body of his book (although he mentions it in the preface) was the existence of commercial plantations and missionaries on the island, and especially the influence that working on the plantations was having on the islanders' social relations. In assuming that they were isolated (when this was no longer the case) and that they were a self-contained society, he presented what was in essence a functionalist picture of Trobriand society. Indeed, he believed that integrated societies made people happier (*Coral Gardens and their Magic*, George Allen and Unwin, 1922, p. 381) and that all social behaviour had to be analysed 'from the functional point of view' (loc. cit., p. 379). In addition, while describing the values which he said influenced Trobriand decisions about production and distribution, he did not ask whether or not everybody accepted these values, or whether these values worked to the clear advantage of some Trobrianders and the disadvantage of others. He did not report anything which might indicate tensions for change in the society. (As a note to this, I should add that when I stayed briefly in the Trobriand Islands in 1976, the community was deeply and violently divided.)

While Malinowski maintained that these societies were

radically different from market societies, the main question for us is whether or not economic and social theory based on the analysis of market societies can be used to analyse societies like the Trobriands where the moral imperative appears to dominate.

A later writer, Karl Polanyi (1886–1964), argued that Western economic and social theory was definitely inappropriate for understanding non-market societies. This is because such theory focuses on problems such as how 'factors of production' like land, labour and capital could be best and most efficiently combined. It had originated in the early nineteenth century to serve the needs of a European society where people increasingly gained their livelihood by selling and buying in the market – in other words, where, as today, you had to buy and sell in order to survive.

In contrast, many non-capitalist societies had not invented or seen the need for things like money, markets, or a clear division of labour. In the Western capitalist societies, important decisions about the amount of land to be used, the supply of labour, the supply of and demand for goods and services, are all regulated through a market mechanism. Where such market mechanisms were absent, the balance had to be achieved in other ways – by moral and ritual means – these being the 'substantive facts' of the society and the economy which give their name to this school of thought.

This approach emphasises the role of values and moral incentives as the wellsprings of human production and distribution, and plays down the profit motive. It is closely related to those views discussed in chapter 1, where the problem of 'development' was seen as being concerned with bringing about a change in people's values.

Formalism

The opposing school is called 'formalism'. It stands in contrast to 'substantivism'. There are variants of this approach. At one extreme there is the view expressed very well in the work of

Raymond Firth. He suggests that there are at least two types of human social behaviour – some is 'economic' and can be analysed using economic theory, but most social behaviour cannot be analysed in this way. There are many areas in which human choices are made in relation to moral beliefs. Such choices are not the outcome of subjective preferences expressed through a market. In these cases, the moral sphere remains dominant, holding back the inclinations to maximise at the expense of others. Thus, what Durkheim referred to as the 'collective consciousness' is the source of social behaviour and the moral community is preserved. But there still remain certain kinds of social relationship which are market exchanges and which can therefore be described by economic theory.

This is a weak kind of formalism. It admits that economic theory is relevant to some but not to all social behaviour. Western economic theory explains only part of social behaviour (see box 5.5).

Box 5.5   *Custom is not the whole story*

'It is sometimes thought that obedience to the social dictates of "custom" inhibits rational calculation. This is not at all the case. In some of the most primitive societies known ... there is the keenest discussion of alternatives in any proposal for the use of resources, of the relative economic advantages of exchange with one party as against another, and the closest scrutiny of the quality of goods in exchanges between groups and taking a profit thereby either in material items or in that intangible good, reputation.'

(Firth, R., in Firth, R. and Yamey, B. (eds.), *Capital, Savings and Credit in Peasant Societies*, Allen and Unwin, 1964, p. 31.)

At the other extreme of formalism are those sociologists and anthropologists who claim that all of social life can be explained by economic theory. All our behaviour is a matter of calculation. We all attempt most of the time to obtain the best bargain in each sphere of our lives – whether that be loaves or loves.

This approach is most clear in the work of P. M. Blau (*Exchange and Power in Social Life*, John Wiley, 1964), who uses concepts such as 'markets', 'supply and demand' and 'price' to describe the maintenance of order and the foundations of power and authority in many areas of social life. He argues that human beings are motivated to gain rewards and use 'social capital' (for example status) to gain their rewards. Thus, for example, if you ask somebody for advice in one situation, you become obliged to them, and are likely to agree with them or support them in another situation. That is the 'price' for the advice. The 'payment' you give them is the power that they now have over you.

What Has This Got To Do With Rural People?

All of this may seem a bit remote from the problem we started with – how do we understand rural society and its place in the process of development? The link is that if we are to understand rural society, we do need to know something of the typical motivations of the people, and also about how they have traditionally organised production and distribution. This is so that we can understand what happens when rural people begin to have social and economic relationships with the worldwide socio-economic system. For those working in the substantivist/ Durkheimian tradition, the problem becomes one of changing the values of rural people so that they will respond to market incentives instead of to traditional values. For those working within the framework of formalist thought, the answer is, surprisingly, not dissimilar in practice. It is to persuade rural people to apply their already developed 'economic' sense to the stimulus of prices rather than, for example, to a desire for social or ritual prestige. In terms of day-to-day development policy, the outcomes are very much the same – to encourage rural people to see that their best interests lie in the adoption of the values of capitalist society. This requires that they produce not for their direct consumption, but for a market, using their cash income to purchase their subsistence requirements in another market.

Policy Implications

These two views of the problem of rural development influenced policy for many years (see box 5.6). To a large extent their influence continues. This is because they are both partially accurate accounts of what is happening in many rural societies in the Third World. But, even together, they remain inadequate.

Box 5.6   *Culture and technological development*

'It comes as a surprise . . . to find that many people in techno-logically less advanced lands are reluctant or unable or accept change with the same ease we do. The wisdom of tradition carries more weight among them, and the cries of "new" and "better" may set people on guard rather than stimulate their desire to experiment. The urge for development and the willing-ness to change are not equally present in all peoples. . . . The factors that determine these motivations are cultural, social and psychological. They may be rooted in the value system . . . they may be associated with the nature of relationships among the members of our group, with problems of status and role . . . they may be found in any number of a vast number of other non-technical contexts. . . . In recent years the existence of human factors in technological development has been increas-ingly accepted. It has been generally recognised that technical experts who work in programs of international aid do better if they understand something about the social and cultural forms of the groups to which they are sent.'

(Foster, G., *Traditional Cultures and the Impact of Technological Change*, Harper and Row, New York, 1962, pp. 4–5.)

However, while culture is undoubtedly important, this view is too restricted. Essentially it sees rural development as 'them' learning from 'us'. It assumes that development is mainly to do with value changes which come about through processes of education or community development. It fails to look at the process of changing values as the outcome not only of changes in individual consciousness, but also of that consciousness within the framework of the developing historical relationship between rural societies and the rest of the world system (see box 5.7).

Box 5.7 *Either/or in theory*

There is an important methodological and theoretical point here. The opposition between the substantivists and the formalists illustrates, that the 'either/or' opposition between theoretical points of view can be very misleading indeed. As we shall see, one of the conclusions that can be reached from new developments which follow the Marxist tradition in sociology, is that neither of the two preceding theories had a monopoly of the truth, and that, paradoxically, the resolution/synthesis of the problem of apparent incompatibility came through the use of another, and in itself apparently contradictory theory, that of Marxism. Marxists say that the problem had been posed in the wrong way. The wrong agenda of questions had been set. If you ask the wrong questions, you get the wrong answers!

Marxist Sociology and Rural Change

The analysis of rural change and peasant society was taken up in great detail by sociologists who informed their research with the ideas of Karl Marx. The following comment by Frankenberg sums up the questions which they thought ought to be asked:

The key questions are: what is produced, by what social groups? How are the groups organised and by whom? What is the purpose of production (use or exchange?). How are the conflicts which arise in the process of production dealt with? What alternative use could be given to the time used in production? If we ask these specifically sociological questions about technological change, two things will follow. First we shall rediscover that the interrelations of technology and society are very complicated, which is no surprise. Secondly, the exogenous comparative statics of cultural evolution can be transformed into a view of dynamic change, initially within individual societies and ultimately to a more sophisticated theory of social evolution.

(Frankenberg, R., Economic Anthropology: one anthropologist's view, in Firth, R. (ed.), 1979, p. 84.)

Summary

In this chapter, we have seen something of the way pre-capitalist, non-market societies first came into contact with the market through imperialism. We have looked at two schools of thought about the sociological understanding of this contact. And we have seen that Marxists think that both are asking the wrong questions. In the next chapter we shall see something of the questions that Marxian sociology asks, and of the answers it provides.

6

Rural development and social differentiation

The problem with the two approaches we looked at in the last chapter is that, while they contain some useful ideas, they do not take into account historical changes, and tend to assume that the societies in which they are interested remain isolated from the rest of the world.

In reality rural society has to be considered as part of a world system and a world history. This is so whether or not a society is obviously part of the wider system (as with plantation agriculture in Africa or Latin America) or less obviously so, as in the case of some parts of Papua New Guinea, where very isolated people use pots and pans manufactured in Taiwan.

The new approach to the study of the sociology of rural societies became influential during the 1970s, partly as a result of criticisms of both modernisation theory and dependency theory, as well as dissatisfaction with both substantivism and formalism. It pointed in a number of directions. In particular it focused attention on the following questions:

1. How does rural society become attached to the wider society? Is there one path or are there several? This problem is sometimes described as the problem of **articulation**.

2. Do classes exist in rural society? Are classes forming in rural society? Are there other kinds of **differentiation** (emerging and institutionalised differences between groups of people) in such societies which are as important as classes? This is sometimes called the problem of differentiation.

3. How is household work organised? Does unpaid household work affect the market prices of cash crops, making them cheaper because household work is unpaid? How is income distributed in rural households?

These questions are very important for the sociology of development, and we shall examine them.

Rural Society and the World System: Lord, Peasant and the State

As one might expect, there are many different ways in which a rural society can become involved with the wider society. In fact we already have two contrasting examples in the case of the Gezira Scheme (box 5.1) and the Arab merchant (box 5.3).

Connection to the world system has often been achieved through force. For example, colonial governments frequently made rural populations pay taxes (see box 5.2). These taxes had to be paid in cash, and the cash could be earned either by working on European plantations, or in urban industry, or by growing export crops on the peasants' farms. The demand for labour for these kinds of work withdrew workers from the family farm. In some cases, as with the Bemba people of what is now Zambia, the decline in production resulted in inadequate diet. The pressure to provide labour in plantation agriculture, or in industry, or to grow cash crops (the prices of which are sometimes kept artificially low by government control of producers' prices) has frequently had this kind of effect on rural populations. In other cases, the effect has been different. For example, in the Highlands of New Guinea, many men have begun to cultivate coffee – which is a very profitable crop. The effect of this has been to enrich the men, who receive the income from the coffee, while the women, who do much of the work, have been burdened with additional work but receive little or nothing in return – the men spending their additional income on their own luxury consumption, and the price of the coffee reflecting the unpaid labour of the women.

Some development projects can have this kind of effect today. In the Gambia, projects with the goal of increasing supply of the national staple food, rice, have resulted in women losing their rights to land, and men in the society gaining a greater control over land and household income than was previously

113

the case. In parts of the Sudan, expansion of large areas of intensive grain production for export has meant that small peasant agriculture has lost land, and nomads have lost access to their traditional grazing lands. One response to these kinds of change is for people to become labour migrants and to leave their land for all or part of the year, exchanging farming for a tenuous life in the urban centres, or on a plantation.

What is common to all these processes is that rural people lose some or all *control* over their production decisions. Often this is the result of state action. Subsistence producers are transformed into new 'social types'. Important among these are 'peasants'. But what is a peasant? Not all the people in rural areas are 'peasants'. You would be wrong to confuse the general terms 'farmer' or 'cultivator' with the specialised use of the term 'peasant' in sociology. The important thing about 'peasants' is that they have to be created – they are part of a social and historical change. When subsistence producers are taxed by the state, and turn to cash cropping to pay their taxes, they become peasants. It is this change from the relative independence of the farmer or cultivator to a relationship with the state which defines a peasant.

The importance of this change should not escape you. In becoming a peasant, a subsistence producer becomes part of a wider society, and enters into new class and status relations. But this is not all. Such people also enter into new political and economic relations in which they are expected to pay taxes, sell crops, provide labour and give allegiance. You may recall that in chapter 2 I mentioned the work of Barrington Moore. The subtitle of his book is 'lord and peasant in the making of the modern world', which emphasises the importance of this vertical link. This new vertical relationship which develops in the process of 'peasantisation' is not an easy one. It is, and has been, the focus of many disputes, riots, strikes, and even wars (see box 6.1).

Box 6.1 *Peasant resistance*

In the 1960s, in Nigeria the cocoa farmers rebelled because they did not consider that the price they were receiving was adequate. The government paid them below the world market price and took the difference as a kind of tax. Dissatisfied, the farmers attacked government offices and personnel.

The Russian revolution of 1917 was at least in part the outcome of peasant dissatisfaction. Attempts at land reform by the Tsarist government had resulted in population pressure on land, indebtedness, and greater poverty than had been usual. There were outbreaks of disorder in 1902 and 1905. Finally, the largely peasant Russian army, fighting against Germany in the First World War, collapsed when the peasants refused to preserve a social order which promised them continuing misery. Eric Wolf in his book *Peasant Wars of the Twentieth Century* (Faber, London, 1971) shows that major revolutions like those in Mexico (1910), Russia (1917) and China (1949), as well as others in the Third World, have been based on widespread peasant discontent, combined with the intellectual and organisational skills of an intelligensia. Clearly, the peasants are a political force of some importance.

Not all peasant opposition takes this dramatic form. It may appear as simple refusal to take the advice of government agricultural officers (reinforcing views that peasants are 'conservative' and don't respond to economic incentives), obscure religious movements which are critical of 'the modern world' and look back to a 'golden age' or forward to future salvation (as in parts of the Pacific and Central Africa), and straightforward theft and robbery of government property.

There are, then, many and various ways in which rural people can become involved in the wider economy and society. Often the effects of this involvement are to increase existing inequality or to introduce inequalities which had not previously existed. It is not that rural societies were utopias of equality (beware of utopias past or future). Indeed in all rural societies there have always been various inequalities of access to valued goods and status. Social and economic differentiation on the basis of gender, age, wealth and ritual status has always been present. Important questions are: What happens when a rural society connects with a world society? How do pre-existing inequalities interact with it? And how does that interaction become the basis for new forms of inequality?

Inequality in Changing Rural Societies

There are two classical approaches to the 'question of differentiation' in rural society. The Russian agricultural economist, Alexander Chayanov (1888–1939), working in the early years after the Russian revolution, based his theories on Russian conditions. He argued that while there were differences in wealth and income in rural communities, they were not absolute differences. What they reflected was the increase and decrease in the amount of labour available in a farm family over the years of its existence (see box 6.2). This combined with a particular system of landholding in pre-revolutionary Russia. Within this system the village community redistributed land periodically according to the needs of different sized families. Similar arrangements are found in some parts of Africa today, for example in parts of Eritrea in north east Africa.

Box 6.2 *Chayanov and peasant household development*

'The family is not . . . a fixed structure, but one which changes over time . . . as an economic entity, a newly-wedded couple setting up on their own would have only two units of labour available. With the birth of successive children, the parents now have additional mouths to feed: the ratio of consumers to workers has deteriorated: the family is in a down-swing phase economically. But children grow up, and begin to help out, at first only in an ancillary way (by minding small animals and helping in the fields) but over time, more significantly. By the age of eight, they can be reckoned as contributing a half-unit of the labour contributed by a mature adult. A family with two teenage sons as well as the labour of the father and mother therefore disposes of four full units of labour. The family is now in the upswing phase.... By year 26 ... 5.2 workers ... feed 6.9 consumers. After that, the family would split, giving rise to new families that would go through the same phases. The parents would then become aged, dependent non-producers themselves, contributing to the adverse worker–consumer ratio of the family now supporting them.'

(Worsley, P. M., 1986, p. 74.)

In contrast, other theorists considered that these factors internal to the household were far less important than the long term forms of differentiation based on ownership of land and capital. Lenin (1870–1924), writing of the development of capitalism in Russia, argued that rural society was developing in a way very similar to that found in the industrial sector of capitalism. In other words, some people were becoming wealthy, capitalist farmers, controlling large amounts of land, using machinery and hiring labour. In contrast, others were losing their land, partly through becoming indebted to the wealthier people, and thus increasingly having to work for cash as labourers on the developing large farms (this is rather like what occurred in Britain in the eighteenth century, see box 1.3).

Lenin thought that this process would continue until rural social structure resembled the class system which classical Marxism saw as the logical development of capitalist development – division into two great classes, the bourgeoisie (or capitalists) and the proletariat (or workers), with irreconcilably opposed interests.

Box 6.3 *Lenin on differentiation*

Lenin's view of the development of inequality in rural society, of 'differentiation', is basically a repetition of Marx's account of the development of class polarisation in capitalist society. He says:

'The system of social–economic relations existing among the peasantry . . . shows us the presence of all those contradictions which are inherent in every commodity economy and every order of capitalism: competition, the struggle for economic independence, the grabbing of land . . . the concentration of production in the hands of a minority, the forcing of the majority into the ranks of the proletariat, their exploitation through the medium of merchant's capital and the hiring of farm labourers.'

(Lenin, V. I., *The Development of Capitalism in Russia* (1899), extract quoted in Harriss, J. C. (ed.), 1982, p. 130.)

Problems appear if we try to apply either of these models to conditions in the Third World. When we try to understand the interaction between local society and culture and the development of capitalist forms of production in say, Africa or South America, the picture is not so clear-cut.

In some cases there does seem to be clearly developing differentiation into an agrarian bourgeoisie and an agrarian proletariat. In the Sudan, for example, some merchants and officials invest their savings in large scale agriculture and employ people to work on their land. However, in many other cases, changes are not so obviously along class lines. Among the Giriama in Kenya, already mentioned briefly in chapter 4, while there have been tendencies towards this kind of division into classes, it is obscured by the continuation of powerful pre-capitalist cultural beliefs about the importance of the status of old people. As we saw in chapter 4, one way out of the moral constraints for intending entrepreneurs is to change religion, become a Muslim, and thus deny the relevance of traditional law to their case. This pattern is quite widespread – and we should recall it as a possible factor in the early relationship between religion and capitalism discussed by Weber in relation to Europe.

In addition, there are complicated mixed arrangements, where a household may do many kinds of work to stay alive. For example, it is not uncommon for some rural household members to spend part of the year working on their own land, part as a labour migrant, part as a sharecropper on somebody else's land, part as a craftworker, and to fill in the remainder by working as a daily labourer on a plantation! (see box 6.4 and reading 1, chapter 10).

Box 6.4   *The case of Hassan Adam*

In 1982, I met a man in the eastern Sudan. He came from 600 km away in the west of the country. There he had some land on which he grew millet, but the development of a large government agricultural project had seriously restricted his farming, preventing him from practising shifting cultivation. Earlier that year he had worked as a labourer on that scheme, and had then sown his millet on his own land, and left it for his wife and children to cultivate. He came east to work as a labourer for a few months on the large farms there. At the end of that time he planned to go to the capital, Khartoum, to see if he could get work as a porter for a few weeks. After that he would return home for the harvest. Hassan was not untypical. Indeed, in the eastern Sudan in October and November, thousands of Hassans with similar stories can be found.

So, although we may use the terms 'peasant' and 'peasantisation', we must be aware of their limitations. Not everybody in rural society is a peasant. And people may have a whole mixture of occupations, and thus of social relations of production, varying from one month to the next and between members of the same household. What we can say is that it is difficult to generalise, and that each case has to be analysed separately. When rural societies come into contact with the wider system, there can be various outcomes.

But, having said this, there does seem to be a general tendency which looks something as follows:

SUBSISTENCE FARMING → PEASANTISATION →
PEASANTISATION + MIXED FORMS OF PRODUCTION →
PROLETARIANISATION + MIXED FORMS OF PRODUCTION →
PROLETARIANISATION

During this process, various forms of social differentiation occur. Some peasants become richer than others, and may turn into entrepreneurs, employing labour, buying land, lorries and tractors. Others may become indebted, lose their land and become wage workers, either on large farms or in cities (see box 6.5).

Box 6.5 *Peasants*

The problem with peasants is that they are always becoming something else. Marx, who had a very poor opinion of them because of their alleged conservatism, considered that they were all alike, 'like potatoes in a sack'. In fact, studies of peasant societies show that they can be loosely divided into rich, 'middle' and poor peasants. Eric Wolf describes these groups as follows:

'The poor peasant or the landless labourer who depends totally on a landlord for the largest part of his livelihood . . . has no tactical power: he is completely within the power domain of his employer. . . . Poor peasants . . . are unlikely to pursue the course of rebellion unless they are able to rely on some external power. . . . The rich peasant, in turn, is unlikely to embark on the course of rebellion. As employer of the labour of others, as money lender, as notable co-opted by the state machine, he exercises power in alliance with external powers . . . (the). . . . Middle peasantry refers to a peasant population which has secure access to land of its own and cultivates it with family labour . . . strange to say – it is precisely this culturally conservative stratum which is most instrumental in dynamiting the peasant social order. This paradox dissolves ... when we consider that it is also the middle peasant who is relatively the most vulnerable to economic changes wrought by commercialism. His is a balancing act in which his balance is continuously threatened by population growth; by the encroachment of rival landlords; by loss of rights to grazing, forest and water; by falling prices and unfavourable conditions of the market; by interest payments and foreclosures ... middle peasants are also the most exposed to influences from the developing proletariat ... (he) ... stays on the land and sends his children to work in the town. ... This makes the middle peasant a transmitter of urban unrest and political ideas.'

(Wolf, E., 1971, pp. 290–292.)

The various mixed forms may represent intermediate stages in the development of new social relations. How long the process takes is difficult to predict. After 200 years, there are still people in Europe who can be described as peasants.

Changes in the Household

One very important way in which contact between rural society and the wider socio-economic system affects social relations is within the household. Chayanov's description of the rural peasant household in Russia emphasised that production decisions were not taken in relation to the market – the aim was to work sufficiently to provide for the members of the household, not to make any great surplus or to sell for a profit. This has often been the case in many peasant households in different parts of the world. As there was little involvement with a wider market system, there was little to buy and thus little requirement to sell. Most of what the household required was produced by itself or within the local community by craft or ritual specialists. Indeed, in many subsistence and peasant societies, if a surplus over household requirements was produced, it was given away or even ritually destroyed.

When households become involved in any kind of wage labour or production for sale, labour itself becomes a saleable item. It has a market value, a price, in other words a 'wage'. When this happens, tensions appear between commitment to the moral community of the family and the local community, and the possibility of individual income and wealth. For example, children who might be expected to work for their father in the fields or herding animals, might now refuse because they could go and earn money by working for someone else. Or the tradition of cooperative work parties may disappear.

The other typical development in this respect is one which has already been mentioned – where a woman or child is expected to work for the household head, according to the old rules of household production, but the household head now sells the product and keeps the money for his (or more rarely her) private use. Sometimes this personal income can be used for luxury consumption, sometimes it can be used in order to buy land or machinery or even to go into business in some way. These kinds of change often affect women quite adversely. All these examples can be understood as a tension between the communal and redistributive values of pre-capitalist societies and the opportunities for private gain offered by production for the market which appear with peasantisation. Subsistence societies in transition to peasant societies, and peasant societies in transition to capitalist or socialist societies, are always riven by such cultural confusions as values change.

Famine, the Green Revolution and Agribusiness

Change is sweeping through the Third World. It takes many forms; often it involves great suffering; sometimes there is gound for optimism as production increases. Why do massive famines occur when elsewhere there is surplus, either within the same country, or in some 'grain mountain' in Europe or North America?

The term Green Revolution was coined in the 1960s to describe the vast potential food grain production unlocked by the selective breeding of new strains of rice, wheat and other food crops. These new strains produce very high yields compared with traditional varieties (see box 6.6). The Green Revolution has increased production very markedly in India and South East Asia, and to a lesser extent in Africa and Latin America.

Box 6.6 *Green Revolution*

A team of scientists working under the direction of Norman Borlaug in Mexico in the 1960s developed some new varieties of wheat known as High Yielding Varieties (HYVs). These:

1. respond very readily to high levels of fertiliser;

2. have short stalks (they do not collapse if the ear of the wheat is very heavy);

3. are very resistant to some common wheat diseases.

There have been similar plant breeding successes with rice. When the new varieties are combined with adequate water, good cultivation and fertilisers the whole package is known as the 'green revolution', a term which presents it as an alternative to a 'red revolution'.

One result of the Green Revolution is that India is now a grain exporter, and in theory has enough food to feed its vast population. I said 'in theory' because people still starve. Why? The answer is that technical change on its own is not a solution. A technical innovation is used socially. In the case of the Green Revolution, not everyone benefits equally. You can see from box 6.6 that the new varieties only work properly if they have enough fertiliser and water. If they do not, their yields may be lower than some of the old varieties which are more drought-resistant. We have seen that peasant society is socially differentiated. The evidence shows that it is the wealthier peasants who have been able to afford the whole package. In doing this they have increased output. They have also expanded their farms and introduced more machinery, pumps and tractors. This has cut down the amount of work available for the poor peasants and landless labourers, who are now probably worse off than before (see box 6.7).

Box 6.7 *Increased differentiation and proletarianisation in India*

In India, that '... the "new technology" has hastened the process of differentiation seems beyond doubt. It has served to consolidate the rich peasantry as a powerful, dominant class: the rich peasantry has become stronger economically and has taken on more of the characteristics of a class of capitalist farmers.'

The degree of proletarianisation has varied:

'... in north-west India we see an incomplete dispossession of the poor peasantry. ... What has happened is that many poor peasants, finding that their small piece of land has become inadequate ... have started to lease it out to rich peasants ... the "new technology" has produced conditions in which ... the poor peasantry are, increasingly, being pushed out of self-employment into wage labour.... But he does retain possession of a piece of land, however small. This has the effect of driving a wedge between the poor peasantry ... and the completely landless wage labourers, making a political alliance between these two classes less easily attained.

A second form of partial transformation may be seen in north-west and other parts of India. ... This relates to sharecropping. There has been a shift from traditional forms of sharecropping ... to cost-share leasing. In the former ... the tenant supplies all the inputs and, in return for the use of the land, hands over fifty per cent of the output to the landlord. ... In the latter ... the landlord supplies the new, bought inputs and, in return

---

takes a far higher share. The sharecropper is close to becoming a pure wage labourer. . . .'

(Byres, T. and Crow, B., with Mae Wan Ho, *The Green Revolution in India*, The Open University Press, 1983, p. 41.)

As well as these unexpected effects, the Green Revolution can also result in poverty in the midst of plenty. While total production rises, production of 'coarse grains' such as barley and pulses, eaten by the poorer people, may actually decline. This has happened in India and Bangladesh. Thus the poor cannot afford the grain produced by the Green Revolution, some of which is actually exported, while their 'coarse grains' become more expensive, and because they have less employment, their incomes may actually fall: a recipe for disaster. They cannot command supplies of food through the market.

Famine

The idea of being able to command food through the market is also useful for understanding famines. We have all seen terrible pictures of people starving in Ethiopia and Sudan. Yet, at the height of the Sudanese famine in 1985, starving people attacked warehouses full of grain.

We are used to thinking of famines as a natural result of drought. But as with many things, from a sociological perspective, the story is not quite so simple. Famines may be set off by droughts, but there are many stops on the road between drought and starvation. One in particular is poverty which prevents people from buying food that is available (see box 6.8).

Box 6.8 *Famine in Wollo, Ethiopia*

There was a terrible famine in Wollo Province, Ethiopia, in 1973. This 'took place with no abnormal reduction in food output, and consumption of food per head at the height of the famine in 1973 was fairly normal for Ethiopia as a whole. While food output in Wollo was substantially reduced in 1973, the inability of Wollo to command food from outside was the result of poor purchasing power in that province. A remarkable feature of the Wollo famine is that food prices in general rose very little, and people were dying of starvation even when food was selling at prices not very different from pre-drought levels. The phenomenon can be understood in terms of extensive entitlement failures of various sections of the Wollo population.'

So, drought did not hit all of Ethiopia, there was not an overall food deficit, and only certain social groups were affected within Wollo. Who were affected?

'Piecing together the available information, the destitution groups in the 1973–4 famine in Wollo would seem to have included at least the following occupational categories (and their dependents):

1. pastoralists. . . ;
2. evicted farm servants and dependents of farmers, and rural labourers;
3. tenant cultivators. . . ;
4. small land-owning cultivators;
5. daily male labourers in urban areas;
6. women in service occupations;
7. weavers and other craftsmen;
8. occupational beggars.'

(Both of these extracts are from Sen, A. K., *Poverty and Famines*, Clarendon Press, 1984, pp. 111–112 and pp. 99–100.)

In Sudan, in 1983–85, one contribution to the famine was the expansion of commercial farming. This took land away from many of the small subsistence cultivators and nomads (remember our labour migrant in chapter 1 and Hassan Adam [box 6.4]). Unable to support themselves, without money, these people starved at least in part because of the expansion of commercial farming as part of 'development projects' encouraged by the World Bank. The wealthy commercial farmers did not starve.

Agribusiness

Worldwide, agriculture is big business run by transnational corporations (see box 6.9). Their interest is in profit, they form an important part of the world system in agriculture as they do in industry (see chapter 4).

Box 6.9 *Agribusiness*

'The subsidiaries of agribusiness transnationals spread across all sectors. They own plantations, management companies, and consultancies, fertilisers and agrochemical plants, animal feed-stuff compounders, sales organisations, shipping companies, insurance brokers and auctioneers, export and import companies, merchant banks, farm equipment distributors, research organisations, factories making processing equipment, food and drink processing companies, packaging and labelling plants, distributing organisations, and even the supermarkets selling the final product. Many of the companies have familiar names, including Unilever, Nestlé, Tate & Lyle, Heinz, Brooke Bond and British American Tobacco.... Even names not generally associated with agriculture – ICI, Hoechst, Shell, BP, all large chemical and oil transnational corporations – are involved in agribusiness activities producing fertilisers, improved seed varieties and agrochemicals, which are among their most profitable activities.'

(Dinham, B. and Hines, C., *Agribusiness in Africa*, Earth Resources Ltd, 1983, p. 9.)

In their search for profit, these companies often establish large plantations which may deprive peasants of their land, in order to grow high value crops for Western and North American markets – those pineapples, mangoes, green beans, bananas that you see in the supermarket are unlikely to have come from small peasant producers. Or, to take another example, very little research is done to find ways of improving subsistence cultivation in the Third World. It is undertaken, instead, to find ways of improving yields of tropical cash crops. The Green Revolution is an example of such research which produced technical innovations suitable for the large scale, wealthier farmers, not for the poor. Often there is a curious link between the type of aid provided by Western governments and the interests of the multinationals (see box 6.10).

Box 6.10   *The World Bank, Nigeria and agribusiness*

'Nigeria's latest plan to increase food production ... was conceived by the World Bank and Nigerian experts. It is expected to cost about US$8.24 billion between 1981 and 1985 and is designed to bring an extra 76,000 hectares under cultivation. Using aid funds, the government will provide financial support, including input subsidies and the provision of rural infrastructure. . . . The vast amounts of money involved in this scheme have galvanised the US business community. With a population fast approaching 100 million, one in four Africans is a Nigerian, and the GNP now far exceeds $50 billion. The government policy is to encourage private enterprise and foreign investment, so profit margins are generous. All this makes Nigeria a prime market for agribusiness transnationals. . . .'

(Dinham, B. and Hines, C., 1983, p. 151.)

Summary

Rural change is complex. Marxian analysis focuses on production relations and the way in which they change. While using the class categories of Marxist theory, division into a proletariat and bourgeoisie, it recognises that there are many other mixed forms of social organisation which appear on the long road from subsistence, through peasantisation to proletarianisation. In this transition, cultural factors can play an important part in determining the result of the interaction between pre-capitalist and capitalist social organisation. The Green Revolution enters into a social environment, and the technology is used to the advantage of some and the disadvantage of others. Famine is as much the result of poverty as it is of drought. While drought is natural, famine is a social process. Agribusiness transnationals, determining agricultural research priorities and production goals, appear to do little to serve the interests of the rural poor. Working with the states and the wealthy of the Third World, they represent yet another aspect of a world system. In the next chapter, we shall look at the state in more detail, and see why and how it serves the interests of the wealthy and rarely those of the poor.

7

State, government and education

In the last two chapters, we looked at some of the differences between market and non-market societies. We saw some of the problems which arose when sociologists tried to understand the relationship between them.

Historically, the transition from non-market to market organisation has been managed by the state. In nineteenth century Europe, it was widely believed that a 'laissez-faire' approach was desirable. The state should act as a kind of referee while entrepreneurs got on with the job of creating wealth through pursuing their individual self-interests. Even so, the state played a major part in the development of capitalism and of industrial society. This took many forms, ranging from the maintenance of a legal system which protected private property and allowed enclosure to occur; which prevented the formation of trades unions; and which later made education compulsory not only because workers wanted education, but also because employers needed workers who could read and write. The state also had considerable influence over the content of education, thus influencing the way people thought and the values they held.

In chapter 2, I indicated that Barrington Moore thought that there had been three routes to development. These were the bourgeois democratic route, the fascist route and the route through peasant uprising. In all these cases, the state played a role. But in the latter two cases, its role was paramount. Japan is the clearest example of a society whose development originated in the total dominance of a ruthless and centralised state accompanied by an extreme nationalist, and also racist, ideology. The Soviet Union and China are examples of largely peasant uprisings in which a centralised state took over the direction of all aspects of production, consumption, distribution, as well as of culture and education.

In most countries of Africa and South and South East

Asia, the Caribbean and the Pacific which experienced colonial rule, the importance of the state was established by the colonising power. In Africa, taxation, forced labour and cash-cropping were all policies which affected rural people as a result of colonial government action (see box 5.2). It should hardly surprise us, then, that in the post-colonial period, the state has continued to be seen as the main force for development. In addition, you may recall that in chapter 2, I mentioned that many of the independence leaders of the Third World were impressed and influenced by the experience of the Soviet Union, which in the period from 1917 to 1956 had become a major world power, had industrialised, launched the first space satellite, improved the health and education of its citizens (many of whom are from the Third World societies of Central Asia) all under the direction of an authoritarian state. These two models, the colonial and the Soviet, in varying mixtures, established the centrality of the state in development – the state is the main force for development in the Third World today. However, we should not imagine that this crucial role is limited to countries outside of western Europe and North America. Today, in the US and Britain, governments which explicitly wish to reduce state intervention in economy and society, in fact pursue policies which deepen and extend that involvement.

Box 7.1 *What is 'the state'?*

The modern European state began its development hand in hand with the development of capitalism. Seventeenth and eighteenth century political philosophers like Thomas Hobbes (1588–1679) and John Locke (1632–1704) tried to make sense of this development as it affected the rights of individuals. The thought of the latter was one of the bases of the laissez-faire view of the state.

When writing of the Third World, sociologists use the term 'the state' in a number of ways. Sometimes, but rarely, they use it to mean 'the government'. More frequently, they use it in two ways, both originating from Marxist sociology. The first

---

may be called the Milliband view, after the writer who first elaborated it (Milliband, R., *The State in Capitalist Society*, Weidenfield and Nicholson, 1969). The second may be called the Poulantzas view (Poulantzas, N., *Political Power and Social Classes*, New Left Books, 1973).

Both these theories are complex and have been the object of much discussion. In this book, I can only give a very brief summary of their views. For Milliband, the capitalist state consists of all the administrative, political and legal arrangements which protect and preserve private property and the power of the bourgeoisie. This weighting of the scales in favour of one class occurs because the personnel of the civil service, industry and banks all share the same kind of educational and family background. They are able to get things done in their way because of the 'old boy network'. Poulantzas adopts a contrasting position. He is clear that the state acts in the interests of the ruling class. However, he emphasises how this happens at an ideological level. The state, he says, sets the ground rules for behaviour through its influence on values in many spheres of life. It influences the form and the content of education, for example, affecting people's consciousness from a very early age. It supports certain views of legality and justice, and through the law it regulates family life, again very fundamental to our perceptions of what is 'right' and 'natural'. It maintains the overall unity of society, but in the interests of the capitalist class and of the capitalist system. In so doing, it is the arena in which conflicts between different sections of the ruling class are resolved.

In contrast to these thinkers, earlier, non-Marxist sociologists such as Durkheim and Weber, paid little attention to the state as a sociological problem, adopting the view that it should be the referee of the laissez-faire society. In modernisation theory, the state was accorded an important place, but as the neutral arbiter and regulator of a developing society. Given the consensus view which underlies modernisation theory, the state could not be seen as other than neutral.

In the last chapter, we saw how the Green Revolution, a rural development policy introduced under state auspices, seems to have served the interests of the wealthy and to have further impoverished the poor. Why should state development policy result in increased poverty for some? How does state policy have these unexpected results, when the state's interest is in 'development'? In this chapter, I want to say more about government and the state and of their role in development. I shall look at education as one example of the relation between the state and development policy.

All governments present their policies as being in the interest of 'the people' or 'the nation'. Most of us are aware that government policy does not in fact work this way – in the developed or in the developing countries. For example, policies which are designed to achieve industrial growth may benefit the owners of factories at the expense of low wages and dangerous working conditions for workers. Another effect may be to hold down prices for agricultural products so that urban workers can have cheap food, but at the expense of low incomes for rural producers.

The problems of the overall regulation of society by government are the concern of the sociology of the state.

Sociological Theories of the State

One commonly accepted theory is known as the 'liberal theory of the state'. This view argues that the state acts in the overall interests of all classes and groups in society. It is a kind of impartial referee, providing the broad services – such as roads, railways, education, the administration of justice – which enable people to get on with their lives. This is not unlike the maintenance of a football stadium, the ground and the provision of the referee and rules, all of which allow the game to be played. It was this view of the state which accompanied laissez-faire capitalism.

Another view of the state is derived from the ideas of Marx and Engels. They proposed two views which can be described as the 'executive committee' model and the 'Bonapartist' model (see box 7.2).

Box 7.2   *Two Marxian models*

The executive committee model

The executive committee model says that the state and government do not act in the interests of all classes in society, but only in the interests of the ruling class – in Marx's own language, the state is the 'executive committee of the whole bourgeoisie'. In this model, the law, education and government policy in general, are all formulated and interpreted in the interests of the 'ruling class'.

The Bonapartist model

Marx also wrote about Louis Bonaparte, better known as Napoleon III of France, who was the leader of a military coup in France in the mid-nineteenth century. Marx wrote about the events of this coup and noted that, in the very particular conditions of that time and place, such was the level of conflict between all the classes in French society that there was a power vacuum. The military stepped into this vacuum and was, for a time, able to govern in its own interests, by manipulating the conflicts between other groups in society.

Another view of the state which is quite similar to the Bonapartist model is that of Milovan Djilas. In his book *The New Class* (Thames and Hudson, 1957), this Yugoslav sociologist argued that, in the Soviet Union, despite a revolution in the name of 'the proletariat' and socialism, oppression and exploitation by the bourgeoisie had been replaced not by proletarian rule, but by the dominance and control of the state functionaries. This group was a 'new class' whose position of dominance was based not on legal ownership of the means of production, but on control of the state's administrative machinery which they manipulated in their own interests.

Some sociologists studying the state in the Third World have tended to take the Bonapartist model as the basis of their analysis. The Tanzanian sociologist Issa Shivji has described the situation as follows:

In an underdeveloped African country with a weak petty bourgeoisie, its ruling section which comes to possess the instrument of the state on the morrow of independence . . . commands enormous power and is therefore very strong. This was precisely the case in Tanzania. . . . The Tanzanian scene . . . comes closer to the 'Bonapartist' type of situation where the contending classes have weakened themselves thus allowing the 'ruling clique' to cut itself off from its class base and *appear* to raise the state above the class struggle. Of course, it is not that the contending classes had weakened themselves in the independence struggle. But a somewhat similar situation resulted from the fact that the petty bourgeoisie was weak and had not developed deep economic roots. This allowed the 'ruling group' a much freer hand. In other words the control of the state became the single decisive factor. For these and other reasons . . . it is proposed to identify the 'ruling group' as the 'bureaucratic bourgeoisie'. Before the Arusha Declaration [a statement made in 1967 by President Nyerere criticising this tendency], this would comprise mainly those at the top levels of the state apparatus – ministers, high civil servants, high military and police officers and such like. One may also include the high level bureaucrats of the Party and the cooperative movement. . . .

(Shivji, quoted in Saul, J., The State in Post-Colonial Society in Golbourne, H. (ed.), *Politics and State in the Third World*, Macmillan, 1979, p. 78.)

Very important questions of development policy are raised by this view. These include whether or not 'development' can be achieved from above, through state action (you should look at some of Nyerere's ideas about this in the extract in chapter 9); and whether or not the taking of political power in the name of 'development' or 'socialism' necessarily involves those who have taken power ultimately governing in their own interests. Above all, the sociology of the state should make us question whereabouts in society 'politics' takes place.

Political Development

Some modernisation theorists (see the extract from Chodak pp. 183–184) have argued that 'political development' means the establishment of states with systems of government akin to those in the developed countries. In contrast, Marxist theorists have emphasised that the existence of the state always means government in the interests of the ruling classes, and that political activity carried on within the institutions of the state is bound to be loaded against the interests of workers and peasants. The following quotation may help you to think about this problem.

Etatism, the identification of politics with the state, developed and flourished as an ideology of the would-be sovereign nation-state. But, while states are a major political force and, given their existence and power, shape any political movement that comes into being, they are not the only political force, or even necessarily the dominant political force in social life.

All the classical questions of 'political philosophy' apply to schools, factories, families, to any human relations: questions of 'obedience', of 'legitimate authority', of 'consent', of 'freedom', of 'justice', of 'democracy', of 'equality', of 'the common interest', and so on. Production of food, for example, can be more or less free, more or less just, more or less demo-cratic. It is not a good sign that the state alone fills the category of 'The Political' when 'the sorts of things it makes sense to say and ask about it' can be said and asked about so many other things and inter-relationships. To those who deny this and claim that the special features of the territorial nation-state constitute it as a philosophically special entity, the question would be: what is the difference?

(Skillen, R., *Ruling Illusions: Philosophy and Social Order*, Harvester Press, 1977, pp. 40–43, quoted in Bernstein, H., Corrigan P. and Thorpe, Mary *Developed or Being Developed?* The Open University Press, 1983, p. 70.)

This view has interesting implications. If 'political' activity is not restricted to the formal institutions of the state, then state-led development strategies are not the only ways forward. You should look at the extract from Julius Nyerere (p. 185), where he says that people have to 'develop themselves'. This does not mean some vague notion of 'working together', but rather taking control of all areas of their lives, including their families, the position of women, the organisation of production, education and culture. Mao Tse-tung (who after all led the development process of the world's largest underdeveloped country, China), put it in the following way:

The socialist revolution on the economic front (in the ownership of the means of production) is insufficient by itself and cannot be consolidated. There must be a thorough socialist revolution on the political and ideological fronts.

(Mao Tse-tung, Fifteen Theses on Socialist Construction, in *On Krushchev's Phoney Communism and its Historical Lessons for the World*, Foreign Languages Press, p. 65.)

What Mao is saying here is that social transformation and 'development' is not only about reorganising production and the creation of plenty; it is also, and most importantly, about people changing the mental and moral world and thus all their relationships with each other – in sum it involves changing what it means to be human.

All these ideas are very abstract. In order to explain them more concretely, we can look at one particular area of sociology, the sociology of education, an area which encapsulates two very important strands: education as a technical process aimed at improved use of human resources in production and thus in 'development', and education as an ideological, moral and political activity.

Education, Ideology and Politics

All societies educate their children. In developed societies, this process, like many other areas of life, has become formalised and rationalised. For the modernisation theorists, there was never any doubt that education was a good thing. Indeed, it would not be going too far to say that for them, education is the royal road to development. It provides skilled people, who become productive 'human capital'. It forms the basis of national consciousness, and thus enables political sophistication.

Culturally, it releases people from the bonds of superstition, enabling them to act rationally rather than traditionally, as Weber might have said. Certainly, within the Third World, education is highly valued both by governments and by people. It is the way forward to economic growth and out of the drudgery of rural life.

As you might expect, dependency theorists did not agree with this assessment. Indeed, for them, the content and form of education in the Third World is seen as another aspect of dependence. Third World education, they say, takes the developed world as its model. It emphasises education of the elites at the expense of the poor. Its content is irrelevant to the needs of poor countries, which require more good farmers and skilled artisans and fewer lawyers, economists, sociologists and physicists. Western-style education deepens and perpetuates dependency.

But, even so, the educational systems of the Third World, established during the colonial period, on European models, are important to people and to governments, and continue to take major portions of national budgets. For the state, education is 'good', even though the link between education, economic growth and development is as yet poorly understood (see box 7.3). For the people, it holds out the promise of joining the elite, getting a 'professional' job, working for the state. There is, then, a clear community of interest between the state and the people in their desire for education. And yet, we have seen that for many sociologists, 'the state' is not a neutral referee in the social football game. It represents class interests. How are these interests furthered by education? Surely mass ignorance is a better guarantee of social order?

Box 7.3 *Education and economic growth*

Ronald Dore, writing about the relationship between education and economic growth in 1976, outlined some of the problems of establishing the relationship between these two variables.

'... it is not until the last twenty years that economists ... have begun seriously to tackle the problem of measuring the precise ways in which, and the precise degrees to which, education contributes to economic growth.

Several approaches have been tried. One ... is the cross-country comparison. If, the argument runs, education contributes to economic growth, then the countries which have had more education should have more economic growth. This is a fascinating game to play. ... The range of variations is infinite. For education, does one choose a measure of primary, or secondary, or tertiary enrolments, or a weighted measure of all three? And should it be enrolments in relation to total population which is easier to measure, or in relation to the relevant age groups which is more difficult? And should it be enrolments, anyway, at a particular time, or school outputs, or the stock of schooled people in the labour force, or should one use some quite different indicator such as the volume of educational expenditure, or an estimate of literacy levels? Economic growth levels, too, can be measured in any number of ways: GNP per capita, the number of kilowatt hours generated, etc. And having settled on the indicators, should one compare enrolments, say, at a given time with per capita income at the same time, or a decade or two decades later, or should one compare enrolments with the rate of increase in income twenty years later – or even the rate of increase in enrolments with subsequent rates of increase in income? And can one usefully refine the analysis by adding some other variable which might be thought to mediate the relation between educational investment and economic payoff, such as, for instance, the degree of egalitarian openness of the educational system, or the level of "political mobilisation" or "political modernity"?'

(Dore, R., *The Diploma Disease*, George Allen and Unwin, 1976, p. 85.)

Education, Opportunity and Inequality

Why do people study and why do governments put so much money into education? One view is that you study in order to be able to 'improve' yourself – which may mean a number of things ranging from being able to improve your future financial position to being a 'rounded person'. Governments, on the other hand, would say that they have to be concerned about the whole society, in particular its level of productivity – all aimed at the common good of present and future generations. To this end, the education system should produce appropriately trained people for the needs of the nation. Education is, then, perhaps the most important place in society within which human inputs are transformed into outputs for society at large: economic growth is assumed to be closely linked to education.

One very important assumption of this view is that 'development' in the developed countries occurred at least in part because of the widespread provision of education by the state. Therefore, investment in education will be a vital part of the development process for underdeveloped countries, and the content of that education – the curriculum – should be similar to that in the developed countries.

The main problem with this train of thought is that it assumes that (a) the development path is the same for all societies, and (b) the content of education should be the same in all societies.

In the developed countries, industrialisation and economic growth were well under way before formal, school-based education became widespread. Universal elementary education was made widely available in Britain only in 1870, and secondary education had to wait until 1902. We have also seen that 'development' in the developed countries did not take place only from within, it also depended very heavily upon inputs of raw materials and labour from the colonial empires. Because of this, any development in the underdeveloped countries is likely to follow a different trajectory – not least because the majority of people in the Third World today live and produce in the countryside, there has not yet been a **'structural transform-**

ation'. In all the countries of the Third World, there is only a very small sector of the economy where people obtain a secure wage through employment in government or private industry. For the largest part of the population, life is dependent on rural production or uncertain employment in the urban 'informal sector'. This means that, for most children, the future does not lie in regular wage employment; neither does it lie in a competitive scramble for individual benefit. And yet, all Third World countries place great faith in education, putting the educational cart before the developmental horse, when in the developed world, education spread in the train of economic growth. But perhaps this is the wrong view of 'education' – education as schooling and qualifications rather than education for self-reliance, education as a way out of cultural, economic and political dependency (see box 7.4).

Box 7.4 *Nyerere on education*

Ex-President Nyerere of Tanzania said that:

'. . . the educational system of Tanzania must emphasise cooperative endeavour, not individual advancement; it must stress concepts of equality and the responsibility to give service which goes with any special ability, whether it be in carpentry, in animal husbandry, or in academic pursuits. And, in particular, our education must counteract the temptation to intellectual arrogance; for this leads to the well-educated despising those whose abilities are non-academic or who have no special abilities but are just human beings. Such arrogance has no place in a society of equal citizens.'

(Nyerere, J. K., *Daily News*, Dar es Salaam, 21 May, 1971.)

Apart from the idea that curricula might be reformulated, away from the contents which were laid down in the colonial era, or which imitate those of developed countries, there is also another point to note. It links to our previous review of the sociology of the state, in particular the state in relation to the rural sector.

   Some years ago, I lived in a small rural village in the Sudan. At the end of the school holidays, when the few boys who had gone away to study at secondary school were preparing to return to school, their elderly aunts and uncles would come to say goodbye. Often in the course of their farewells, these relatives would say 'Please God, may you become an official'. This little phrase encapsulated a whole system of beliefs about the role of education and its place in the state. It said that social worth was to be achieved by occupying a position in the state, and that gaining examination diplomas was the way forward to success and 'knowledge'. But more than this, it was also what the state itself said in the way that it provided education, in the content of that education, and in the incentives that it held out. Ronald Dore has described this as 'the diploma disease' (see box 7.5).

Box 7.5 *The diploma disease*

'Unfortunately, not all schooling is education. Much of it is mere qualification-earning. . . . Everywhere, in Britain as in India, in Russia as in Venezuela, schooling is more often qualification-earning schooling than it was in 1920, or even in 1950. And more qualification earning is mere qualification-earning – ritualistic, tedious, suffused with anxiety and boredom, destructive of curiosity and imagination; in short, anti-educational . . . for the . . . school systems of the countries of the Third World . . . (this) . . . becomes a disaster. Primary schools which serve chiefly to give the majority of their pupils the label 'failed dropouts': secondary schools and universities which seem designed to squeeze every ounce of curiosity and imagination out of a man before he is discharged into the bureaucracy to take responsibility for his country's destinies; growing armies of secondary and university graduates for whom no slots can be found in the bureaucracy, and – despite these growing numbers of educated unemployed – relentless and growing pressures for

---

> more secondary schools and universities to 'widen opportunity':
> such, in the developing countries ... are the consequences of
> using schools as the chief means of sifting each generation into
> those who get the prize jobs and those who don't, and of letting
> that sifting function dominate – even it seems to obliterate –
> the school's ancient function of providing education.'
>
> (Dore, R., 1976, pp. ix–x.)

Such a 'diploma disease' has certain social effects. It
reinforces a view of society which emphasises academic
education and the superiority of mental as opposed to manual
work; it emphasises that academic education should be along
the same lines as in the developed countries; and as the state
is run by people who have come through the path of academic
education, it reinforces their 'success', the legitimacy of their
wealth and their power, in contrast to the 'failure', poverty and
powerlessness of those who never went to school or did not
gain any diplomas at all. These are all part of the 'hidden'
ideological content of education, and (Marxist sociologists of
the state would argue) one of the ways in which the state serves
the interests of the dominant classes – legitimating their position
through this idea of education. There is, then, a link between
the state, education, ideology and power. In order to get a job
which has status, income and power, you need to learn the
educational 'rules'. Very often this does not only mean learning
the ideas and values appropriate to an 'educated' person, but
learning them in a foreign language, perhaps English, French,
Portuguese or Arabic because these are the languages of the
elite.

Inevitably, then, education and inequality are closely
linked. Within countries, there may be unequal educational
expenditure between regions. Within regions, different social
groups may have differential ability to send their children to
school. And within households, girls are less likely to be sent
to school than boys, and boys are likely to be encouraged to
stay on as long as possible. The state sets the rules, but not

everyone has the same chance of learning them, or of entering the game. To put this another way, and to bring out the relation between education, the state and politics more clearly, education can be seen as empowering some people by initiating them into the 'secret language' and culture of the elite, while ensuring that the rest see themselves as failures because they were not 'able'. If people believe that they failed because they were not good enough, they are likely to accept their own powerlessness as right and proper. In this way, at an ideological and cultural level, the state can exercise control. Some might say that this kind of education is a cheaper and more effective means of repression than guns and water cannon!

Education and Freedom

Despite some similarities, Dore and Nyerere really have very different approaches. For Dore, the problem with education in the Third World (and in the First and Second Worlds of 'the West' and 'the Eastern block') is that it is not really education, it is training and disciplining. It is not aimed at encouraging curiosity, but at selection. The problem for Dore is not with schooling as such, but with what goes on in schools. For Nyerere, the problem is different. His concern is not only with the appropriateness of the curriculum for his country, but also with changing people's values to those more suited to a cooperative and socialist society. He is concerned with moral education. Thus, for him, education is explicitly a political activity – it should establish the values which he considers necessary for a socialist society. A number of questions might be asked of both of them. These are: 'do either of these views of education really empower people to make their own lives?', 'Is Dore merely lamenting the demise of an elitist education which has never been available to any but the elite and which will still divide people into failures and passers?', 'How can we be sure that Nyerere's values, or those of the Minister of Education are in the interests of the masses of people whom education is supposed to benefit?'

Education and Empowerment

In contrast to Dore and Nyerere, Ivan Illich, Everett Reimer and Paulo Freire consider schooling as something bad, and formal education as a means of repression. All of them implicitly use the Marxist concept of 'false consciousness' to explain what education is usually about. For them, education should take place outside of schools, and should be an activity which provides people with intellectual and cultural power to resist the depredations and demands of unjust states. For Illich, in particular, education is a way of deepening the dependency of the powerless on the powerful. His answer is to 'deschool' society, to take education (and as a matter of fact, health-care) out of the state's control and make it available in other ways (see box 7.6).

Box 7.6   *Illich on schooling and deschooling*

'Why we must disestablish schools. . . .

Many students, especially those who are poor, intuitively know what schools do for them. They school them to confuse process and substance. Once these become blurred, a new logic is assumed: the more treatment there is, the better are the results; or, escalation leads to success. The pupil is thereby "schooled" to confuse teaching with learning, grade advancement with education, a diploma with competence, and fluency with the ability to say something new. His imagination is "schooled" to accept service in place of value. Medical treatment is mistaken for health care, social work for the improvement of community life, police protection for safety, military poise for national security, the rat race for productive work. . . . Not only education but social reality itself has become schooled. . . . Rich and poor alike depend on schools and hospitals which guide their lives, form their world view, and define for them what is legitimate and what is not. Both view doctoring oneself as irresponsible, learning on one's own as unreliable, and

145

community organisation, when not paid for by those in authority, as a form of aggression or subversion. . . . Everywhere not only education but society as a whole needs "deschooling". . . . The poor have always been socially powerless, the increasing reliance on institutional care adds a new dimension to their helplessness. . . .'

(Illich, I., *Deschooling Society*, Penguin, 1975, pp. 9–11.)

For Illich, deschooling society means recognising that most of what people learn is absorbed outside the classroom. Therefore, education should take place throughout life, through 'learning webs' (informal and demand-fed arrangements where willing learners and willing teachers meet by mutual arrangement). Perhaps Illich's ideas are too radical, interesting for what they make us think about our own educational experience, but in the end more suited to societies with high standards of living, removed from the basic struggle for existence characteristic of most of the Third World. One might think this, but Paulo Freire, although differing in detail from Illich, follows a similar line. The difference is that he is and has been a practitioner. Prior to going into exile from his native Brazil in 1964, he was Secretary of Education and General Coordinator of the National Plan for Adult Literacy. His approach was unorthodox, and unpopular with the military government which came to power in 1964, partly because of its emphasis on literacy and education as empowerment, on enabling people to break out of their false consciousness and see the possibilities which they have of taking control of their own lives – a process which he calls 'consciencisation'.

By and large, the ideas of Illich, Reimer and Freire have had little effect on educational policy and practice in the Third World. They may have influenced some of the rhetoric, but Dore's picture of the situation is substantially more accurate as an account of how things are. Education in most countries is highly selective, favours the wealthy, and holds out the prize of a job in the 'modern' sector. School enrolments have increased dramatically. Literacy has risen. But most people 'fail', and most resources go into secondary and higher education. Only in a very few countries has adult literacy been made a priority. For the rural and urban poor, and particularly for girls and women, education offers little except confirmation of their powerlessness and 'failure'.

Summary

In this chapter I have explained how the state has been central to 'development' and economic growth. This centrality continues in all the countries of the Third World. While modernisation theory saw the state as a kind of social referee and governor, Marxist sociologists have seen the state as a problem, asking in whose interests it acts. Whose interests do state policies support? I have used the example of education policy to show that there are serious problems with the content and form of education in the Third World, and that despite the radical theories of Illich, Reimer and Freire, there seems little hope of improvement. Education, in their sense, or even in the sense in which Dore uses it, can present a serious threat to state power.

8

Gender and development

Men usually despise occupations manned [sic] predominantly by women, be it agriculture or trade, and they will normally hesitate to take part in such work.

(Boserup, E., *Woman's Role in Economic Development*, George Allen & Unwin, 1970.)

Gender and Inequality

Women make up more than 50 per cent of the world's population, and yet in every country, without exception, their social position is inferior to that of men. What this means in practice is that they work longer hours, have poorer educational opportunities, poorer health care, less control over their lives. This chapter looks at the position of women in development.

In recent years, a lot of research has been done by women working within a feminist approach. Feminism is not only a social and political movement aimed at improving the position of women. It is a set of theories, a new language (see Spender, D., *Man Made Language*, Routledge and Kegan Paul, 1980, for more about this), for talking about the world. It begins from the assumption that history and society can be such as looked at from the viewpoint of women, where previously the male perspective has dominated and excluded that of women. Some feminists have argued that although the unequal treatment of women can be partially explained by Marxist sociology, such as looking at women's relations to the means of production, such an approach does not go far enough. For this reason, they have rejected Marxist theory. Instead they argue that in all societies, women are subordinate to men. This subordination is not something which appears with the development of capitalist society. It is found in all societies. It is true of subsistence farming societies in which women take the major part of the work load and receive (along with children) the least return, as well as in societies such as the Soviet Union or China, where despite the disappearance of capitalist production relations, women receive lower wages than men, and occupy fewer positions of influence.

In response to this evidence, some feminists suggest that the real problem which must be understood is '**patriarchy**' – the general relationship whereby women are subordinated to men in all places and times (see box 8.1).

Box 8.1 *Patriarchy and class*

Feminists have seen the problem of patriarchy in the following terms. Historically, groups who rule by birthright are fast disappearing. They are increasingly being replaced by societies in which social class is the main basis of social differentiation, and within which there is usually some possibility for movement between classes. However, there remains one ancient, immobile and universal scheme for the domination of one birth group by another. This is the scheme that prevails in the area of sex. The political power which men wield over women amounts to the fundamental political division in society. Western society, like all other civilisations, is a patriarchy in which the rule of women by men is more rigorous than class stratification, more uniform, certainly more enduring. In capitalist society, the domination of women by men is obscured by class differences between women. In fact, such class differences are transitory and illusory because whatever the class of her birth and education, the female has fewer permanent class associations than does the male. Economic dependency renders her affiliations with any class a tangential, vicarious and temporary matter. This implies that class divisions are relevant only to men. Significant class differences do not exist between women. There is a more fundamental system of domination – patriarchy. This is independent of capitalism or any other form of society.

[In this section, I have paraphrased and elaborated upon some paragraphs from Barrett, M., *Women's Oppression Today*, Verso Editions, 1984, p. 11.]

What do you think is meant by the phrase: 'Economic dependency renders her affiliations with any class a tangential, vicarious and temporary matter'?

Not all feminists would agree with the view expressed in the paragraph above. Indeed, the importance of patriarchy in explaining the position of women is still the subject of heated debate.

Women as Consumers and Producers

One way of looking at the subordinate position of women is by comparing their educational opportunities with those of men. Literacy is a good indicator of access to education; it is also an indicator of a wider potential for participation in society. One very basic problem that women face is their apparent 'invisibility'. By this I mean that their experience is often assumed to be adequately described by statistics dealing with men, and that accounts of society given by men tell us adequately about the lives of women. The less educated women are, the less likely they are to be able to make their views and feelings public. Thus literacy is an important indicator of their ability to obtain their needs in society.

Box 8.2 *Women's literacy*

Morris (see chapter 9) presents information about literacy rates in 73 countries. The literacy rate measures the percentage of the adult population of a country who are able to read and write to at least some basic level.

In only six of the 73 countries with which Morris deals do women have a higher literacy rate than that of men. In very few is it equal; in most, the women's rate is very considerably lower than that of men.

In chapter nine we will look at the Morris's Physical Quality Of Life Index (PQLI), a composite measure of development. This index is made up three components. Literacy is one of them. The other two are life expectancy at age one and infant mortality. In general, the life expectancy of women is greater in all societies than that of men. The *World Development Report* for 1985 (International Bank for Reconstruction and Development, Washington, 1985, table 23) shows this to be the case for all but five of the 126 countries on which it presents information. The five exceptions are: Nepal, India, Pakistan, Bhutan and Papua New Guinea. In a fifth country, Iran, the rates are the same. The facts that in general women live longer than men, and that female infant mortality in the first year of life is lower than that of males, means that the PQLI should actually be weighted in their favour.

Overall, the comparison between male and female PQLI scores shows that there are 28 countries in which the PQLI is lower for women than for men, even though the calculation of the PQLI is weighted in favour of women in the ways that I have indicated. In 18 countries, this difference is particularly large. Table 1 (page 152) shows how this result comes about.

Table 1 shows that, although in many cases the life expectancy and infant mortality indices are more favourable to women than to men, women's overall scores are pulled down by their poor scores on the literacy index. If the PQLI were expanded so as to take into account additional measures such as hours of work, illness, access to health care, access to credit for investment purposes, and many other possible indicators, then the gap between men and women in their consumption of the goods and services produced in any society, would, I suspect, be consistently larger.

Because national statistics are rarely collected specifically about women, it is difficult to find out about their position. In

Table 1 *Physical Quality of Life Index, selected countries*

Country	Date	Total PQLI score	Female	Male	Diff. (F–M)	Life expect. index F	Life expect. index M	Inf. mort. index F	Inf. mort. index M	Literacy index F	Literacy index M
Algeria	1964	36	34	38	–4	43	37	52	47	8	30
Burma	1962	45	40	49	–9	37	31	44	37	40	80
Cameroon	1965	24	20	28	–8	8	5	45	48	7	31
Cyprus	1960	82	80	85	–5	87	76	85	90	64	88
Egypt	1960	42	39	45	–6	56	48	51	56	9	32
Greece	1961	84	82	86	–4	91	83	86	84	70	92
Hong Kong	1960	76	74	79	–5	83	63	86	83	52	90
India	1970	40	35	45	–10	42	44	41	44	22	45
Indonesia	1971	49	47	51	–4	42	37	50	44	49	71
Jordan	1961	54	48	61	–13	52	52	77	81	15	50
Liberia	various	26	21	31	–10	38	36	21	41	4	14
Malaysia	1970	67	65	69	–4	59	51	87	82	50	72
Pakistan	1966	35	32	38	–6	37	40	51	44	7	29
Peru	1961	58	55	62	–7	53	51	64	60	48	74
Sri Lanka	1969	80	78	82	–4	79	75	84	80	72	89
Thailand	1949	55	52	59	–7	44	36	76	72	36	69
Turkey	1971	55	52	59	–7	70	63	51	43	34	69
Zambia	1969	33	30	37	–7	20	11	37	38	35	61

(Morris, M. D., *Measuring the Condition of the World's Poor*, Pergamon, 1979, pp. 84–5.)

many cases such separate data is not collected. Nowhere is this clearer than when we look at women's contribution to production. Often, this has to be obtained from case study material rather than from broader statistical information.

In her book *Subject Women* (Fontana, 1982), Ann Oakley discusses such a case study of the Tanulong and Fedilizan peoples who live in the Philippines. She notes that:

In industrial-capitalist societies, there are three main forms of productive activity: that geared to goods that will be *directly used*, that which leads to goods for *exchange*, and that which ... results in the cyclical reproduction of labour power. ... The last of these is an important domain of female labour. ...

(Oakley, A., 1982, p. 138.)

In non-industrial societies, women make very considerable contributions to production of goods that will be directly used and to the 'cyclical reproduction of labour power' – which means domestic work, caring for children, men, animals, houses.

Among the Tanulong and Fedilizan people, some 60–80 per cent of food is produced by women (see box 8.3). Such a contribution is not unusual. In a study of the participation of women in farm work in a number of Asian countries, Boserup found that women put in between 41 and 76 per cent of the amount of the farmwork done by men *in addition* to their domestic work (Boserup, E., 1970, p. 25).

Box 8.3 *The gender division of labour among the Tanulong and Fedilizan*

This table [adapted from Bacdayan (1977)] shows the distribution of tasks between men and women in Tanulong and Fedilizan. Of the 50 tasks listed, 80 per cent are done equally by men and by women, only 18 per cent are done exclusively by men. Even so, a very large proportion of the total food produced and consumed is the result of women's work. Such a massive contribution of labour does not appear in the official statistics. This is because it is work which has been done either for direct consumption or for 'the cyclical reproduction of labour power'. None of this work is counted in the figure for Gross Domestic Product (GDP) (see box 9.2) because none of it is sold on the market.

Agriculture or subsistence tasks

Preparation of the soil	B
Planting	B
Weeding the banks of the fields	B
Plowing with animals	M
Weeding in between the rice plants	FM
Watering	B
Erecting scarecrows	MF
Guarding against rice birds	B
Trapping rats and mice	M
Installing magical objects to scare rats	B
Checking to see if rice is ready for harvest	B
Harvesting	B
Sowing seeds	F
Removing seedlings from seedbeds	B
Clearing upland fields	MF
Planting vegetables	B
Clearing the padi dikes	FM
Fertilising with organic matter	B
Planting beans	FM
Installing bean poles	FM
Gathering beans	FM
Weeding upland sweet potato fields	FM
Fencing	B
Building stone/earth walls	MF
Fixing dikes	B
Fertilising with mineral soil	B
Planting sweet-potato vines	FM
Digging up sweet potatoes	FM
Preparing upland fields	B
Taking care of animals in the pasture	MF

Cutting grass for animals	MF
Cutting sticks for fencing and poles	B
Preparing bamboo for binding rice bundles	MF
Milling sugar cane	B
Hauling rice from the fields	MF
Digging up new upland fields	B

Search for food

Fishing in the river	MF
Trapping birds	M
Gathering mushrooms	M
Snaring rice birds	M
Trapping fish in the rice fields	MF
Gathering edible snails	FM
Gathering beetles	B
Hunting	M

House-building tasks

Gathering thatch roofing	B
Roofing	M
Gathering vines for binding	M
Preparing wood	M
Preparing the ground for building	B
Hauling the material to building site	B

B = tasks performed equally by females or males; F = tasks performed by females only; M = tasks performed by males only; FM = tasks performed usually by women; MF = tasks performed usually by men.

'You might like to think whether such under-reporting of women's work is restricted to the Third World. In particular, think about the following. When a woman cares for a sick person in hospital, we call her a nurse and pay her. When she does the same work at home, we call her "mum" and don't pay her. In the former case, her work is counted as part of the GDP, in the latter it is not. Why?'

(Oakley, A., 1982, pp. 140–141.)

Women and Development

We have seen that women and men do different work. They have different status. The division of labour and social status are closely related. Thus, doing different work from men, women are treated differently. This different treatment is the result of the different *value* which is placed on their work. Sometimes women's relatively high status can be lowered as development occurs (see box 8.4).

Box 8.4 *Development and !Kung women*

(The ! before the k in !Kung, represents a click sound which is found in some of the languages of Southern Africa.)

Ann Oakley describes a typical way in which 'development' affects women, using the case of the !Kung people of the Kalahari desert in Southern Africa studied by Patricia Draper. She says:

'A transformation in the nature of the economy radically alters women's relation to their work. The traditional economy of the !Kung bush people . . . allotted an important role to women as agriculturalists providing the staple food supply . . . in the late 1960s some . . . (of the people) . . . were beginning to adopt a more settled way of life with men taking up herding and the women agriculture. This change from a nomadic foraging exist-ence was accompanied by marked changes in the social relations of the sexes and definitions of gender roles. In the bush setting . . . women have a higher degree of autonomy and power within the community. When economic conditions alter to a settled way of life centred on animal husbandry and crop planting, relations between the sexes become asymmetrical and women lose their independence. The most important factor accounting for this revision of women's place is their relation to work. In the bush setting they are independent workers and retain control over the product of their labour (food). They are just as mobile as men and no more tied to the home: their travels outside the

---

village to get food give them an acquaintance with bush life
(the location of animals, water etc.) that is of enormous political
importance, since it makes them the unique possessors of
knowledge crucial to the community's survival. When life
becomes more settled, the men, through herding and participation in waged work outside the village, develop a pattern of
absence, while the women become more bound to the home.
Consequently, men come to 'carry an aura of authority and
sophistication that sets them apart from the women and
children'. . . . At the same time, domestic chores multiply: food
preparation becomes more complex, material possessions
proliferate, houses become more permanent and private. The
egalitarianism with which children were reared gives way to an
emphasis on gender-differentiated responsibilities: boys,
expected to help with the herding, regularly move out of the
village, whereas the lives of girls are more narrowly defined by
the cycle of female domestic activities.'

(Oakley, A., 1982, pp. 139–142.)

One very important way in which women are affected
by development stems from their 'invisibility' to planners and
politicians. Although they often do a very large amount of the
farming in rural societies in the Third World, when development plans are being made this is forgotten. New land is cleared
and given to men to grow cash crops; credit arrangements are
designed so that men receive the money; agricultural extension
services are aimed at men. In many cases, as in that of the
!Kung, development actually works to further disadvantage
women. As consumers of development, women find that their
already subordinate position is made worse by loss of land and
exclusion from new ideas. In this way they are often made
dependent on men in ways which were not previously the case.

Box 8.5 *Development can increase women's dependence on men*

'One major problem is that, where labour-saving technologies are introduced which apply to women's work, they have been handed over to male control. Small implements such as presses, grinders or cutters have been given or sold on credit to men by development agencies, even when the work for which they are a substitute is traditionally done by women. For example, corn grinders have been made available in Kenya but women are not taught to operate them. Oil presses in Nigeria, tortilla-making machines in Mexico, and sago-processing machines in Sarawak are also purchased and operated by men, partly because only they have access to cash or credit. There is a very high demand for food-processing machinery from women, but without control of the equipment they are able to relieve the pressure of work only by continuing reliance on men's machines, which involves spending any cash they can save for this purpose. The situation helps to reinforce the stereotype that women cannot manage machines, and that they can only cope with the most low-productivity and low-value operations.'

(Rogers, B., *The Domestication of Women*, Kogan Page, 1980, p. 173.)

Sex Discrimination in Sociology

Women experience discrimination when consuming and when producing. The example of literacy (see table 1) shows that they are less likely to consume education at the same rate as men. They are also more likely to drop out of education. The way that women's unpaid domestic and farm work is not usually counted in national statistics (see box 9.2) shows how their work is often 'invisible' to government. These are both examples of how the subordinate position of women is likely to be reinforced because we all (including many women) tend to look at society through the eyes of men. Remember that not one of the founders of sociology to whom I have referred in this book was a woman – they are often called the 'founding fathers'. Indeed, with the notable exception of Engels (who wrote about the family, and thus had to say something about the position of women), not one of them even wrote about women. This reflects discrimination against women in the Western world. The processes of discrimination against women in the academic world has biased our view of the Third World. Male social scientists have tended not to write about women. With some very notable exceptions, such as Margaret Mead, very few women anthropologists and sociologists interested in the Third World have risen to prominence. Inevitably, then, the pictures which we have of these societies are usually men's pictures. A male anthropologist or sociologist is likely to spend most of his time talking to men – particularly in societies where women and men lead very separated lives. This fact is a very important example of research bias which profoundly limits our understanding of society both in the Third World and in our own world, and which, like all sociology of development, should make us think very hard about our own society as well as about others.

Sex and Gender

'Sex' is a biological term – it describes physical differences between people. 'Gender' is a sociological term – it describes differences in social behaviour. This is an important distinction because we tend to confuse the two, and in this confusion, to assume that social differences are *caused* by physical differences. There is considerable evidence to suggest that the physical differences between males and females are not such as to account for the observed differences in social behaviour and social roles (for more about this, see Rose, S., Kamin, L. and Lewontin, R., *Not in our Genes*, Penguin Books, 1984). Forms of explanation like this are called 'reductionism' (see box 8.6).

Box 8.6 *Reductionism*

'. . . the name given to a set of general methods and modes of explanation both of the world of physical objects and of human societies. Broadly, reductionists try to explain the properties of

---

complex wholes – molecules, say, or societies – in terms of the units of which those molecules or societies are composed. They would argue, for example, that the properties of a protein molecule could be uniquely determined and predicted in terms of the properties of the electrons, protons, etc., of which its atoms are composed. And they would also argue that the properties of a human society are similarly no more than the sums of the individual behaviours and tendencies of the individual humans of which that society is composed. Societies are "aggressive" because the individuals who compose them are "aggressive", for instance. In formal language, reductionism is the claim that the compositional units of a whole are . . . prior to the whole that the units comprise. That is, the units and their properties exist *before* the whole, and there is a chain of causation that runs from the units to the whole.'

(Rose, S. et. al., 1984, pp. 4–6.)

Many everyday explanations are reductionist. But so are some sociological explanations. McClelland's idea of Nach (see chapter 1 and box 4.1) is an example, as is Spencer's whole sociology (see box 1.9). Some, but not all, Marxist theory, which tries to explain everything in terms of the 'economic base', is another example.

Much recent research has provided evidence that gender roles can vary radically between societies. Although the debate continues (for a well-argued and fascinating contrary view, see D. Freeman, *Margaret Mead and Samoa*, Harvard University Press, Cambridge, Mass and London, 1983), it is now widely accepted that gender, the way that we behave as men and women, is predominantly part of our culture rather than part of our biology (see box 8.7).

Box 8.7 *Gender and culture*

'The individual comes into the world with no set notion of what male and female are, but develops this classification process at about two years of age; subsequently this is elaborated and used as a way of making sense of the social world and guiding action. Precisely what characteristics the child will use for distinguishing between appropriate and inappropriate action for his or her gender will depend on cultural influences. Hence the *content* of the internal reference value, the gender role concept, depends on external influences; but the existence of the potential for classifying and acting on the basis of categories such as male or female is something which is part of the human biological make-up. In this way, human beings possess the intellectual equipment for incorporating aspects of their culture into a particular way of viewing the world, one which emphasises differences between categories. One might almost say that people are "programmed" to look at the social world in terms of differences, and that gender provides the most readily available material for this programme to act upon. The construction of this internal gender reference system occurs gradually throughout development without the child being consciously aware of it. Eventually, he or she comes to regard their own culturally induced variety of gender differences as equivalent to the natural order of things. In other words, nurture becomes second nature.'

(Archer, J. and Lloyd, B., *Sex and Gender*, Penguin Books, 1982, pp. 211–212.)

We saw in chapter 1 that a 'scientific' theory of social evolution was used to legitimate imperialism. With biological, reductionist theories of human social behaviour, we are seeing a similar process, whereby 'science' is used to support the status quo where men have power and influence over women. Sociology as a science must take little for granted, and must ask questions about the sociology of scientific beliefs. As I said in chapter 1, it questions things in such a way as to make the familiar unfamiliar and the unfamiliar familiar. In the same way that:

The theory of evolution is not just an inert piece of theoretical science. It is, and cannot help being, also a powerful folk tale about human origins.

(Midgley, M., Origin of the Specious, *New Statesman*, 22 November, 1985, p. 23.)

so biological theories of social behaviour must be approached critically by sociology. The sociological approach always demands that we ask of theories, 'whose interests do they further and whose interests do they undermine? What kinds of folk tale are they?'

Naturalisation

Evolutionary theory applied to social behaviour served the interests of the white citizens of the developed world. Biological theories of human social behaviour serve the interests of men. When it is said that women in Taiwan and South Korea are particularly suited to the assembly of computer chips, because as women they are *biologically* more suited to such work, being fast, delicate and accurate in their work, we see an explanation which manages to be simultaneously reductionist, biologistic and racist. As an explanation, it entirely omits any consideration of the social and political position of women in those countries. It fails to take into account the pressures which make them, rather than men, available for such work. These include the fact that they are cheaper to employ because they are 'unskilled' or 'semi-skilled', that they have poorer education, and that they are not protected by labour legislation (see box 8.8).

Box 8.8 *Women as skilled workers*

'The famous "nimble fingers" of young women are not an inheritance from their mothers in the same way as they may inherit the colour of her skin or eyes. They are the result of the *training* that they have received from their mothers and other female kin since early infancy in tasks socially appropriate to woman's role. For instance, since industrial sewing of clothing closely resembles sewing with a domestic sewing machine, girls who have learnt such sewing at home already have the manual dexterity and capacity for spatial assessment required. . . . It is partly because this training, like so many other female activities coming under the heading of domestic labour is socially invisible, privatised, that the skills it produces are attributable to nature, and the jobs that make use of it are classified as "unskilled" or "semi-skilled".'

(Elson, D. and Pearson, R., The Subordination of Women and the Internationalisation of Factory Production, in Young, K., Wolkowitz, C. and McCullagh, R. (eds.), *Of Marriage and the Market*, CSE Books, 1981, pp. 149–150.)

What evolutionism and biologism have in common when applied to society is that they 'naturalise' social behaviour – making it seem that what happens in society has been 'scientifically' demonstrated to be natural, and therefore unchangeable. Such a view is seriously questioned by sociology (boxes 8.6 and 8.7 both indicate why this 'naturalisation' presents difficulties as a way of explaining social behaviour).

Gender and Politics

Once you begin to see gender roles as cultural, as the result of what we *believe* rather than of what we '*are*', you can begin to ask questions about how far they can be changed, and under what circumstances. Women do behave differently in different societies; this fact gives us some idea of the *ranges* of different behaviours, social roles, which are possible. Feminist theory has argued that insofar as women's position in society is not 'natural', so it is also something which can be changed. Change involves questioning the accepted 'truths' of society, and thus also the established positions of those who benefit from those 'truths'. Because of this, change is a very political activity. In the case of the position of women in development, that politics is about gaining power so as to shape societies better to meet the needs of 52 per cent of the world's population. Such change will inevitably affect the position of men, and does and will involve many kinds of 'politics', ranging from the slow but sure pressure to ensure that women are educated, receive adequate health care for their special needs, get access to credit for their farming, to the more spectacular political demonstrations sometimes associated with the 'Women's Movement' (see box 8.9). In the end, it requires a change of values and of the way in which both women and men see the world. It is not a matter of a few initiatives to 'improve the position of women' while leaving power, authority and status firmly in the control of men. It is a matter, as with all oppressed groups, of empowering them to take control of their own lives, economically and culturally.

Box 8.9 *Policies for women*

'This is the point that needs impressing upon all those policy advisers, policy makers, policy implementers, at national and international levels, who wish to "include women in development", "enchance the status of women" etc. The single most important requirement, the single most important way of helping, is to make resources and information available to organ- isations and activities which are based on an explicit recognition of gender subordination, and are trying to develop new forms of association through which women can begin to establish elements of a social identity in their own right, and not through the mediation of men. Such organisations do not require policy advisers to tell them what to do, supervise them and monitor them; they require access to resources, and protection from the almost inevitable onslaughts of those who have a vested interest in maintaining both the exploitation of women as workers, and the subordination of women as a gender. The most important task of sympathetic personnel in national and international state agencies is to work out how they can facilitate access to such resources and afford such protection – not how they can deliver a package of readymade "improvements" wrapped up as "women's programmes".'

(Elson, D. and Pearson, R., 1981, pp. 165–166.)

What has Happened to Women in the Third World?

It is undoubtedly the case that colonialism and development have changed the lives of women in the Third World as they changed much else. Colonial governments did introduce education for women, they did attempt to protect women from some very unpleasant experiences such as female circumcision. But, at the same time, they had their own ideas as to how women should behave and what work it was appropriate for them to do. The social transformations wrought by capitalist development are always ambiguous. Is it better to be the ignorant, secluded wife of a wealthy farmer or a literate woman working long hours in a factory? Is it better to be the wife of a poor farmer, or the wife of a labour migrant, receiving only occasional remittances, and bringing up a family and cultivating a smallholding alone? These questions are difficult to answer. Whatever the answer, changes are under way, although they may merely swap one kind of gender subordination for another (see box 8.10).

Box 8.10 *Gender subordination: intensification, decomposition and recomposition*

Elson and Pearson point out that employment of women in factory, 'modern sector' work, can represent three ways in which their subordination to men can be 'intensified', 'decomposed' or 'recomposed' as development occurs. They say:

'One example of the way existing forms of gender subordination may be *intensified* is the case of a multi-national corporation operating in Malaysia which believes in deliberately trying to

preserve and utilise traditional forms of patriarchal power. . . .
The economic value of daughters certainly provides a motive
for fathers to exert more control, including sending them to
work in the factories whether they wish to or not. . . .'

'. . . As an example of the way existing . . . gender subordination
may be *decomposed*, we can cite . . . the importance of factory
work as a way of escaping an early arranged marriage in some
Asian countries. In . . . a society dominated by the capitalist
mode of production, "free-choice" marriage is two-edged . . .
marriage tends to take on the characteristics of the dominant
form of choice in such societies, a *market* choice from among
competing commodities. And it is women themselves who take
on many of the attributes of the competing commodities, while
it is men who exercise the choice. This tendency towards the
recomposition of a specifically capitalist, "commoditised" form
of making marriages is actively encouraged by the management
styles of some of the large American multi-national electronics
companies which provide lessons in fashion and "beauty care"
and organise beauty contests and Western-style dances and
social functions for their employees.'

'. . . Though one form of gender subordination, the subordination of daughters to their fathers, may visibly crumble,
another form of gender subordination, that of women employees
to male factory bosses, just as visibly is built up. Work in world
market factories is organised through a formal hierarchy with
ordinary operators at the bottom controlled by varying levels of
supervisors and managers. In study after study the same pattern
is revealed: the young female employees are almost exclusively
at the bottom of this hierarchy; the upper levels . . . are almost
invariably male. . . . This *recomposition* of new forms of gender
subordination in which young women are subject to the authority of men who are not in any family relation to them can
also have the effect of intensifying more traditional forms of
gender subordination.'

(Elson, D. and Pearson, R., 1981, pp. 157–159.)

Worldwide, there are differences in women's position both materially and culturally. Eating last, after the men and boys of the family have finished the meal which you have prepared, is one form of inequality found in some parts of Africa, the Middle East and India. But so also are the limitations placed on the movements and careers of wealthy middle class women by the ideology of *machismo* in the rich suburbs of Sao Paulo in Brazil or Buenos Aires in Argentina. In the Islamic world (which stretches from Morocco in the West to Indonesia in the East, via Egypt, Pakistan and Soviet Central Asia), religious edict commands that women are not equal to men, and should be protected and disciplined by them. The Koran says:

Men have authority over women because Allah has made the one superior to the other, and because they spend their wealth to maintain them. Good women are obedient. They guard their unseen parts because Allah has guarded them. As for those from whom you fear disobedience, admonish them and send them to beds apart and beat them.

(*The Koran*, translated by Dawood, N. J., Penguin, 1968, pp. 360–361.)

Such edicts can have ambiguous social interpretations. The separation of women can enable them to live their own lives, oppressed and within strict bounds, but nonetheless perhaps a better life than as a 'modern' woman, as the following account of 'Eve-teasing' in non-Islamic, urban India shows:

'Eve-teasing (physical and verbal molestation of women) and rape are manifestations of . . . the attitude which denies us our humanity, which reduces us to mere objects: mere bodies to be used or abused.

If these bodies are not on piecemeal sale for a few rupees, or life-time sale with a dowry thrown in, then they can be trespassed on, and sampled at will. If they are not the well-guarded property of one man, then any man is free to buy them if he can, or grab them if he can't.

And this man is not necessarily a pervert, a "goonda". He could be the respectable elderly gentleman who edges closer to you in the cinema; anonymous hands pinching you in the bus; a boyfriend who expresses his love for you by "screwing" you or any girl who comes his way, while his father keeps a virgin bride ready for him. He is often our employer, whose molestation we have to put up with to hold the job; the landlord whose fields we cultivate, the policeman we go to for help. . . . Eve teasing . . . is a way of spitting out contempt at us for being women. And this is true whether the remark hurled at us is "Hello, Sweety" or an obscenity. . . . It is a systematic attempt to destroy our sense of self . . . sexual violence is a conscious process of intimidation to keep women oppressed and in a permanent state of fear.'

(Editorial in Manushi, *A Journal About Women and Society*, New Delhi, quoted in Leghorn, L. and Parker, K., *Woman's Worth*, Routledge and Kegan Paul, 1981, pp. 152–153.)

In East Asia, the Confucian tradition is also clear about the inferior position of women. Within this tradition, several hierarchies – old to young, rulers to ruled, men to women – are assumed to be the 'natural' order of society. Even so, women enter the labour market, but because of their inferiority, they end up with a double burden, child-care, domestic work and a job – everywhere in the world, 'a woman's work is never done' (see box 8.11). In Latin America more than elsewhere in the Third World, many women do manage to follow careers. Often though, they can do this only because of the other cheap women workers whom they can pay to do 'their' domestic work. Society (not only in the Third World) is full of such ironies, and nowhere more than where gender and class inequalities overlap.

Box 8.11 *The double burden: while men play, women pay*

'The Ethiopian peasant woman . . . begins her day far earlier and ends it far later than her husband and children, in order to do all the work that permits men extra sleeping and socialising time. Asian women working on plantations must work full-time the year round as housewives, and as labourers during the growing season, while their husbands enjoy leisure time after plantation work is over. Women in the North Indian tea-gardens work two to four hours more each day (not including their housework) than their husbands. Husbands of Mazahua migrant women in Mexico City often stop working altogether when their wives' trade is lucrative. They may help carry crates for their wives, but at other times they simply relax or socialise with other men. Chinese husbands in many agricultural communes enjoy leisure time during their lunch hours that is made possible at the expense of their wives, who must do food preparation and childcare during this time. Their situation is not too different from that of the husband and wife who work in Industry City, USA, and return together, whereupon he sits back with a beer and TV show, eating dinner, then goes out with "the boys", while she prepares the dinner, cleans up and puts the kids to bed.

Studies of the total number of hours worked weekly by men and women (that claim to include all of women's domestic work) in Asian and African villages show this discrepancy. In the Philippines women worked sixty one hours to men's forty one and Ugandan women worked fifty hours to men's twenty three. In only two out of ten sample villages did women work the same number or less hours than men; and it is doubtful that all of women's childcare and home maintenance work was recorded.'

(Leghorn, L. and Parker, K., 1982, pp. 193–194.)

In societies which have espoused the revolutionary path to development, there have usually been explicit and sustained attempts to improve the position of women. In such countries, the situation is very uneven. Despite the rhetoric, men are still usually firmly in control. In the Islamic countries, such as Algeria, the veil and seclusion are still very apparent. In others, such as in Soviet Central Asia and South Yemen, there have been marked changes. Another aspect of the unevenness concerns domestic labour. In the Soviet Union, there may be many women doctors and engineers, but they are still expected to carry the double burden by their menfolk. In conditions of revolutionary war, as in Vietnam, women may bear arms and fight alongside men. But when the war has been won, gender 'normality' may return. In Eritrea, in northern Ethiopia, where the people are fighting for independence from Ethiopia, I have seen women carrying Kalashnikovs, and fully equipped to enter combat alongside the men. But I have also noticed that when there is food to prepare and serve, it is usually they who do it. However, perhaps, it is a matter of priorities. For in rural Eritrea, the revolution has certainly improved women's lot. Relations between these men and women are changing. Women do not have to be forced into arranged marriage, can have land and can control the product of their labour. Certainly, when I was there in 1985, International Women's Day was widely celebrated and dramatised, while back in Britain it went largely unnoticed!

Summary

In this chapter we have seen that women are subordinated in all societies. This subordination is not 'natural', but cultural. The 'founding fathers' of sociology did not write about women except as part of 'the family', and this invisibility continued until feminist researchers began to make them visible. Their research shows that development can affect women in ambiguous ways, but, by and large, their subordination only changes its form. Perhaps the really major development which has to take place in human society is the empowerment of women.

Part Three

THEMES IN THE
SOCIOLOGY
OF DEVELOPMENT

9

Defining and measuring development

Problems of Defining Development

You might have expected me to discuss this problem in chapter 1, together with a neat definition of development. There is a very good reason for having left it until this stage. By now you should have realised that 'development' is a concept which is full of value judgements in general, and political value judgements in particular. This is true of much of the subject matter of sociology. It is even difficult to decide on the precise words that we should use to describe the 'underdeveloped', 'developing', 'less developed', 'backward' parts of the world (see box 9.1).

Box 9.1 *Definitions, descriptions and theories*

Here are some of the words which are frequently used to describe the characteristics of those countries and areas which might be described as 'underdeveloped'.

poor	undeveloped
tropical	traditional
backward	overpopulated
less-developed	physically underdeveloped
developing	industrialising
black	rural
underdeveloped	Third World

You might like to think about three questions in relation to each of these characteristics:

1. What assumptions does each one make about the nature of the 'development process'?

---

2. How far is each of the words useful as a general label for particular countries? In other words, how *general* is it?

3. What political or other values might be implied by using any one of these terms?

In thinking about these questions, you should remember what I said in chapter 1 about theories being like languages, and languages allowing us to talk about some things and not others, about the way that words set the agenda for discussion. You should look at table 2 (below), ignoring for the moment the column headed PQLI.

Table 2 *Measurement of Gross National Product per capita and Physical Quality of Life Index, in 150 countries*

Rank in per capita GNP among 150 countries	Per capita GNP ($)	PQLI	Cumulative population (thousands)
1. Kampuchea	70	40	7,585
2. Laos	70	31	10,718
3. Mali	90	15	16,090
4. Bangladesh	92	35	86,809
5. Ethiopia	97	20	113,224
6. Rwanda	97	27	117,164
7. Upper Volta	99	16	122,872
8. Nepal	102	25	134,774
9. Burma	105	51	164,268
10. Burundi	111	23	167,826
11. Somalia	111	19	170,806
12. Chad	113	18	174,638
13. Malawi	115	30	179,276
14. Guinea-Bissau	120	12	179,782
15. Benin	124	23	182,662
16. Guinea	126	20	186,831
17. Lesotho	131	48	187,927
18. Niger	132	13	192,231

19. India	133	43	770,406
20. Zaire	136	32	793,468
21. Afghanistan	137	18	811,597
22. Gambia	153	25	812,083
23. Tanzania	154	31	826,438
24. Pakistan	155	38	891,943
25. Haiti	176	36	896,337
26. Sri Lanka	179	82	909,587
27. Yemen Arab Rep.	180	27	915,805
28. Vietnam	189	54	957,084
29. Indonesia	203	48	1,084,840
30. Sierra Leone	203	27	1,087,654
31. Madagascar	204	41	1,095,130
32. Kenya	213	39	1,107,379
33. Central African Emp.	226	18	1,109,080
34. Comoro Islands	230	43	1,109,368
35. Sudan	241	36	1,126,350
36. Egypt	245	43	1,161,786
37. Togo	250	27	1,163,890
38. Yemen, People's Rep.	260	33	1,165,438
39. Uganda	265	40	1,176,018
40. Cameroon	273	27	1,182,135
41. Mauritania	287	17	1,183,358
42. Nigeria	297	25	1,242,357
43. China, People's Rep.	300	69	2,047,679
44. Western Somoa	300	84	2,047,832
45. Botswana	316	51	2,048,486
46. Thailand	318	68	2,087,405
47. Bolivia	332	43	2,092,500
48. Mozambique	333	25	2,101,237
49. Philippines	342	71	2,142,258
50. Swaziland	353	35	2,142,697
51. Equatorial Guinea	354	28	2,142,995
52. Senegal	355	25	2,147,167
53. Honduras	359	51	2,149,962
54. Zambia	415	28	2,154,621
55. Liberia	415	26	2,156,237
56. El Salvador	432	64	2,160,049

Rank in per capita GNP among 150 countries	Per capita GNP ($)	PQLI	Cumulative population (thousands)
57. Morocco	436	41	2,176,364
58. Jordan	452	47	2,178,848
59. Papua New Guinea	460	37	2,181,413
60. Korea, Rep.	464	82	2,213,748
61. Grenada	465	77	2,213,854
62. Congo	465	27	2,215,122
63. Cape Verde	470	48	2,215,404
64. Ecuador	505	68	2,221,965
65. Ivory Coast	506	28	2,226,563
66. Colombia	526	71	2,250,546
67. Rhodesia	529	46	2,256,338
68. Albania	530	75	2,258,664
69. Paraguay	533	75	2,261,138
70. Guatemala	540	54	2,266,852
71. Mauritius	552	71	2,267,714
72. Guyana	559	85	2,268,464
73. Ghana	595	35	2,277,715
74. Angola	601	16	2,283,727
75. Tunisia	626	47	2,289,169
76. Dominican Rep.	630	64	2,293,900
77. Cuba	640	84	2,302,923
78. Nicaragua	650	54	2,305,067
79. Syria	662	54	2,311,820
80. Malaysia	692	66	2,323,100
81. Peru	701	62	2,337,387
82. Algeria	780	41	2,352,948
83. Turkey	789	55	2,390,505
84. Lebanon	822	79	2,393,174
85. Taiwan	847	86	2,408,598
86. Costa Rica	884	85	2,410,464
87. Brazil	912	68	2,512,931
88. Fiji	989	80	2,513,480
89. Mexico	996	73	2,568,239
90. Iraq	999	45	2,578,451
91. Jamaica	1,037	84	2,580,407
92. Malta	1,050	87	2,580,727

93. Romania	1,100	90	2,601,438
94. Chile	1,137	77	2,611,249
95. South Africa	1,205	53	2,634,331
96. Panama	1,240	80	2,635,899
97. Guadeloupe	1,240	76	2,636,241
98. Iran	1,260	43	2,666,882
99. Uruguay	1,268	87	2,669,914
100. Surinam	1,282	83	2,670,311
101. Argentina	1,285	85	2,694,877
102. Yugoslavia	1,341	84	2,715,724
103. Barbados	1,352	89	2,715,966
104. Bahrain	1,370	61	2,716,198
105. Cyprus	1,481	85	2,716,851
106. Portugal	1,535	80	2,725,546
107. Martinique	1,540	83	2,725,897
108. Reunion	1,550	73	2,726,367
109. Hong Kong	1,624	86	2,730,451
110. Netherlands Antilles	1,642	82	2,730,685
111. Bulgaria	1,780	91	2,739,327
112. Trinidad and Tobago	1,867	85	2,740,309
113. Singapore	2,111	83	2,742,471
114. Gabon	2,123	21	2,742,984
115. Greece	2,148	89	2,751,846
116. Venezuela	2,171	79	2,763,232
117. Hungary	2,180	91	2,773,668
118. Puerto Rico	2,230	90	2,776,491
119. Ireland	2,354	93	2,779,534
120. U.S.S.R.	2,380	91	3,028,437
121. Spain	2,485	91	3,063,043
122. Poland	2,510	91	3,096,200
123. Italy	2,756	92	3,150,494
124. Bahamas	3,284	84	3,150,684
125. Czechoslovakia	3,330	93	3,165,232
126. Saudi Arabia	3,529	29	3,173,585
127. Israel	3,579	89	3,176,773
128. United Kingdom	3,658	94	3,232,727
129. German Dem. Rep.	3,710	93	3,249,853
130. Japan	4,146	96	3,357,579

Rank in per capita GNP among 150 countries	Per capita GNP ($)	PQLI	Cumulative population (thousands)
131. New Zealand	4,222	94	3,360,505
132. Libya	4,402	45	3,362,602
133. Austria	4,529	93	3,370,095
134. Finland	4,984	94	3,374,724
135. Australia	5,449	93	3,387,905
136. Netherlands	5,558	96	3,401,221
137. France	5,585	94	3,453,013
138. Iceland	5,708	96	3,453,224
139. Belgium	5,845	93	3,462,966
140. Luxembourg	6,054	92	3,463,307
141. Norway	6,221	96	3,467,249
142. German Fed. Rep.	6,507	93	3,528,440
143. Canada	6,527	95	3,550,364
144. Denmark	6,606	96	3,555,342
145. United States	7,024	94	3,764,744
146. Sweden	7,668	97	3,772,911
147. Switzerland	8,569	95	3,779,312
148. Qatar	11,779	31	3,779,492
149. Kuwait	13,787	74	3,780,415
150. United Arab Emirates	14,368	34	3,780,735

Source: taken from Morris, 1979.

The problem of defining 'development' is an example of what Gerry Rose (*Deciphering Sociological Research*, Macmillan, 1982) calls the 'concept indicator link'. Rose says that it is necessary to be careful about moving from the general level of abstract ideas, words which do not always have very clearly defined meanings – like development – to the level of measurement, where it is important to define our terms carefully so that we can use them as measures. He says:

Many of the theoretical concepts used in sociology (e.g. social status, conformity, alienation, authority) are images of reality, abstractions which are not observable directly. To investigate a proposition like ... (urbanisation causes a breakdown of traditional beliefs) ... we must define empirical indicators for the concepts. The process of developing an indicator and testing

its validity is often called 'operationalising' a concept; sometimes this is done through the use of . . . (a) . . . scale.
(Rose, G., 1982, p. 305.)

So, although we are unlikely all to agree on precisely how to define development, because we may have different value positions, this is not a major problem. Max Weber said that all scientists (not only social scientists) start off from personal value positions. The real scientific problem is to undertake research in such a way that the form of the argument, the definition of the concepts, the method of measurement, is made clear to others. It is for this reason that the 'concept-indicator link' is very important in any scientific or logical argument.

Gross National Product (GNP) and the Measurement of Development Using the Physical Quality of Life Index (PQLI)

You will have seen in table 2 that the wealth of a country can be measured by GNP per capita (per head). This measure is a mean average. It says nothing about the distribution of total income. Thus, some countries such as Kuwait and Qatar, with very unequal income distribution, may have the highest GNPs per head in the world. In contrast, the People's Republic of China has a much lower average, but a more equal distribution. Economists usually measure the degree of inequality by means of a 'Gini coefficient'. Another measure of national wealth is GDP (see box 9.2).

Box 9.2 *GDP and GNP*

As well as GNP, we sometimes use another measure of wealth. This is Gross Domestic Product (GDP). This concept adds together all economic activity taking place within a country. GDP per head is calculated by dividing the total value of economic activity by the total population.

In contrast, GNP tells us the value of the economic output resulting from the use of resources – labour, land, capital – owned by *national* members of the society.

179

The distinction between GNP and GDP is important. Many Third World countries are heavily dependent on foreign capital. If foreigners invest in a country, they want to take some at least of their profits to their home country. The outflow of profits from some countries can mean that GDP may exceed GNP by up to 20 per cent. The main foreign investors in the Third World are very large transnational or multinational companies (see box 6.9).

The Physical Quality of Life Index (PQLI): a Measure of Development

Obviously, 'development' is a very complex concept. It can be defined in many different ways, depending on which characteristics of individual people's lives or whole societies you consider important. You might use GNP, for example, if you decide that the level of overall productivity of the entire society is the main feature of a developed society.

M. D. Morris, in his book *Measuring the Condition of the World's Poor* (Pergamon Press 1979), attempts to develop an index of the 'physical quality of life'. Morris says that constructing such an index is difficult because it involves comparing very different societies. He says that a useful measure must meet the following conditions:

1. It must not assume only one pattern of development. In particular, it must not assume that the Western way is the only way.

2. Related to (1), the measure must not assume that the values of 'development' are the same in all societies.

3. The measure should measure *results* (how many people can read and write), rather than *inputs* (how much has been spent on education).

4. It must reflect the distribution of social benefits. It should not use mean averages which may disguise serious maldistribution of benefits.

5. It should be simple – complex indicators are difficult to understand.

6. It should enable comparison between countries and regions of countries.

Inevitably, it is difficult to meet all these criteria. But Morris suggests that it is possible to construct an index using three indicators – life expectancy, infant mortality at age one, and adult literacy. His PQLI for a country is the mean of any country's scores on these three indicators.

If you look at table 2, you will see that Guinea-Bissau (country no. 14) has a PQLI of 12. This suggests that the quality of life for people there is very poor. In contrast, Sweden (country no. 146) has the highest PQLI, at 97. You may have noticed in table 2 that there is no clear relationship between GNP per capita and the PQLI. Box 9.3 discusses why this might be so.

Box 9.3 *PQLI and GNP*

'The variation among groups of countries in terms of income and the physical quality of life measure ... is not entirely surprising. Poor countries (those with low per capita GNPs) tend to have low PQLIs, while higher income countries tend to have high PQLIs.... In fact, however, the correlations between GNP and PQLI are not all that close. While deviations exist at all levels of income, they are particularly evident at the upper and lower ends of the per capita income range.

At one end of the spectrum, the oil producers of the Middle East, most particularly Saudi Arabia, Qatar and the United Arab Emirates and Libya, stand out with high per capita GNPs and low PQLIs.... Of these high income oil-states, only Kuwait has a relatively high PQLI of 74. Four of the five countries have incomes equal to or above the average of all high income countries; yet three have PQLIs below the average of the poorest countries – and Libya's PQLI is only marginally higher than that of the low income countries.

Other gross deviations in which PQLI is quite low relative to GNP include Angola (where GNP is $601 and PQLI is 16) and Gabon (where per capita GNP is $2,123 and PQLI is 21). Although Iran has a per capita GNP ($1,260) more than nine times larger than India ($133), its PQLI is no higher.

If nothing else, such examples show that "money is not everything".'

(Morris, M. D., 1979, p. 60.)

The PQLI shows up some of the problems of measuring development along one axis, even when you use a composite index. It is, though, limited in its usefulness. Streeten and Hicks have summed up some of the problems (see box 9.4).

Box 9.4 *Some problems of the PQLI*

'A recent study of the use of a composite index ... Morris's ... PQLI uses three simple indicators with equal weights to attempt to measure the fulfilment of "minimum human needs".... Morris argues that the use of indicators for judging performance under basic needs criteria should concentrate on outputs or results rather than inputs. Input measures, he feels, do not measure success in meeting the desired goals, and may lend an ethnocentric bias to the means employed. The use of only three indicators permits the calculation of the PQLI for a wide range of countries and facilitates the examination of changes in the index over time. The term "quality of life" is perhaps a misnomer, since what is really being measured is effectiveness in reducing mortality and raising literacy. Life expectancy measures the quantity, not the quality of life.... Most importantly, the weighting system of the PQLI is arbitrary and there is no rationale for giving equal weights to literacy, infant mortality and life expectancy at age one. It is not possible to prove that PQLI gives a "correct" index of progress on human needs, as opposed to some alternative index having different weights or a different selection of component indices. It is not clear what is gained by combining the component indices with a weighting system that cannot be defended.'

(Hicks, N. and Streeten, P., Indicators of Development: the Search for a Basic Needs Yardstick, in Streeten, P. and Jolly, R. (eds.), *Recent Issues in World Development*. Pergamon, 1981, pp. 61–62.)

Development as a Value

In chapters 1 and 2, we saw how values often underlie socio-logical development theory. I now intend to look at some of the ways in which this comes out in the work of various writers. In particular, I want to look at two aspects of this: first of all how 'scientific' jargon can *disguise* values; and secondly how some contemporary development 'experts' – those politicians who have tried to achieve development – have understood 'develop-ment' as being about more than those parameters which, for example, Morris tries to measure.

Development as 'Growing Systemness'

The following extract from Szymon Chodak is an example of the way in which sociological jargon can be used to make the problem of development seem a 'scientific', value neutral, technical problem.

I propose to view societal development as a growing systemness ... this is not an entirely new idea ... it is contained in numerous classical writings, especially ... the works of Marx, Tonnies, Durkheim, Weber.... In my understanding, when development refers to societies, it implies an entwining of numerous and variant threads of separate processes of develop-ment and of separate structures, entities, groups, units and agencies. These are constituents of the general development, but they simultaneously take their form from their own consti-tutive threads. Separate threads and processes of development, though related and affecting each other, are not necessarily congruent and hence do not necessarily change at the same pace ... the process of development as discussed here can be characterised as a continuity occasionally interrupted or stalemated, yet nevertheless irreversibly directed toward greater complexity. Thus it is a process which generates wider and larger systems and densifications of intrasystemic interdependencies. It is a process which engenders systems of higher levels while engulfing systems of smaller capacity. Tonnies describes it as an emergence of *Gesellschaft* which absorbs the variety of *Gemeinschaft*. Durkheim characterises it as a growing organic solidarity superseding mechanical solidarities in a more complex division of labour. Today these processes are even more complex and, what is especially important, they are becoming engulfed by even wider processes regulated and coordinated by the modern state through networks of bureaucracies. Thus societal development generates eventually the need for etatisation.

(Chodak, S., *Societal Development: five approaches with conclusions from comparative analysis*, Oxford University Press, New York, 1973, pp. 8–9.)

In this extract, Chodak sees development as a process by which societies become more complex. This is a theme, as he notes, taken up by most of the classical sociologists. Increasing complexity means that small scale societies join together into large scale societies and the new, larger social system requires regulation by a larger political unit – the rise of the nation state, what Chodak calls 'etatisation'.

You may like to read the extract carefully and try to work out Chodak's value position. There is a clue in the way he sees the state. You may like to refer back to the section on the sociology of the state in chapter 7.

Development as Development for, by and of the People

Julius Nyerere, the first president of Tanzania, writes as a politician and not as a social scientist. Since its independence in 1961, Tanzania has been the focus of a determined attempt to develop 'African socialism'. The country has faced many difficulties, and the development effort cannot at present be judged as successful. However, this is in part because of Nyerere's radical vision of development, which involves the participation of the people and the more equal distribution of wealth. In this extract, he talks of development as the realisation of human potential.

A country, or a village, or a community, cannot be developed; it can only develop itself. For real development means the development, the growth, of people. Every country in Africa can show examples of modern facilities which have been provided for the people – and which are now rotting unused. We have schools, irrigation works, expensive markets, and so on – things by which someone came and tried to 'bring development to the people'. If real development is to take place, the people have to be involved. . . . For the truth is that development means the development of *people*. Roads, buildings, the increase of crop output, and other things of this nature, are not development; they are only tools of development. A new road extends a man's freedom only if he travels upon it.

(Nyerere, J., *Freedom and Development*, Oxford University Press, Dar es Salaam, 1973, p. 25 and p. 59.)

Development as Leaving Tradition Behind

The next extract, by S. N. Eisenstadt, written in the same apparently technical and neutral prose as Chodak, argues that 'development' involves a transition to 'modern' forms of socio-economic organisation and thought. Such a transition is necessary because 'traditional' societies are limited in their imaginativeness and openness to change. This is so because they are dominated by narrow ideas which constrain all forms of creativity. For this reason, change must come from outside.

Traditional societies, whose analysis has been of crucial importance in studies of modernisation, are of special interest. . . . The societies that have been designated as traditional vary widely, from the so-called primitive societies to the differing literate societies . . . and many other types of societies.

Whatever the differences between different traditional societies, they all share the acceptance of tradition, of the givenness of some actual or symbolic past event, order, or figure as the major focus of their collective identity, as the delineation of the scope and nature of their social and cultural order and as the ultimate legitimator of change and of the limits of innovation. . . .

It is these cultural definitions of tradition as a basic criterion of social activity, as the basic referent of collective identity, and as the delineator of the definition of the societal and cultural orders – of the symbols of collective and personal identity and the degree of variability among them – that constitute the essence of traditionality.

(Eisenstadt, S. N., *Tradition, Change and Modernity*, John Wiley and Sons, New York, 1973, pp. 151–152.)

Eisenstadt's discussion of traditional society and its transition to modernity is typical of the modernisation approach. Durkheim's influence on this approach should be apparent to you. It invites us to ask the following questions:

1. Is it useful to describe such a wide range of societies – 'the so-called primitive societies to the differing literate societies' – by one theoretical idea, 'traditional society'?

2. Is the USA a traditional society because it takes the Constitution as a 'major focus of . . . collective identity'?

3. What values underlie the way in which the term 'modern' is used?

At base, modernisation theory asserts that there is only one path to development, the European way. This path can be repeated through cultural and institutional change under state auspices. It does not consider it relevant to look at the detailed history of Third World societies, recognising the changes which have occurred within them as they became linked to the wider world.

Development as a Struggle Out of the Status of Being 'Third World'

Another definition of development identifies the position of Third World societies in the world system as being part of their problem.

[Third World societies are]. . . . All those nations which, during the process of formation of the existing world order, did not become rich and industrialised. A historical perspective is essential to understand what is the Third World, because by definition it is the periphery of the system produced by the expansion of capitalism.

(Abadalla, I–S., *Que es el Tercer Mundo* [What is the Third World], in Guia del Tercer Mundo (Guide to the Third World), 1981, Mexico, Periodistas del Tercer Mundo, p. 6, quoted in Thomas, A. and Bernstein, H., *The Third World and Development*, Open University Press, 1983, p. 20.)

This view of Third World societies recognises that problems of development do not arise exclusively from internal constraints within a society. They have much to do with a society's position within the world capitalist system. Samir Amin, a Third World writer, says:

Underdevelopment is manifested not in the level of production per head, but in certain characteristic structural features that oblige us not to confuse the underdeveloped countries with the now-advanced countries as they were at an earlier stage of their development.

(Amin, S., *Uneven Development*, The Harvester Press, 1976, p. 201.)

Amin distinguishes the following three features of the Third World in relation to the rest of the world:

1. Third World societies are mainly primary producers, and cannot control the prices of their products.

2. What is produced in the Third World is determined by demand for primary produce from the developed countries.

3. The Third World does not have the concentration of industrial and technological developments of the developed countries.

Taken together, all these factors mean that 'development' in the Third World cannot follow the same path as in the developed countries. Indeed, their development is likely to be 'uneven', with surprising juxtapositions: nuclear physics and bullock carts (as in India), capital intensive farms and subsistence producers (as in Zimbabwe), huge motor car factories and hunter-gatherers (as in Brazil). This in turn suggests that the sociology of development has to concern itself with the study of new, and unexpected forms of social and economic organisation which are not always taken account of by theories which build heavily on the past experience of the developed world. It is concerned not only with the present, but very much with the future.

Development Alternatives

The sociology of development does not ask questions only about the Third World. It also poses many questions about society in the First World (the capitalist countries) and the Second World (the centrally planned countries of Eastern Europe). In part, it poses these questions because the subject itself has had to make sense of a rapidly changing world situation in which the superiority and 'rightness' of European and American society, politics and culture is increasingly questioned. Robin Cohen sums up these points when he looks at some of the broader reasons why modernisation theory came to be seen as inadequate, in particular after the defeat of the United States in Vietnam in 1973 (see box 9.5).

Box 9.5 *Development and developed societies*

... it was changes in the external world that served to crack ... modernisation theory.... Let me identify here only two major shifts in consciousness. First, a largely peasant nation, Vietnam, had stood up to the global power of the United States, and ... had defeated it. Technological and material superiority was henceforth to be thought of as inferior to 'winning the hearts and minds of the people', to use a phrase of the times. Second, within the core industrialised societies, there was a spiritual and moral crisis popularly referred to as the growth of a counter-culture ... which questioned the trajectory and purpose of a society based predominantly on the cash nexus. Interestingly enough, the models that were assembled for cultural recognition and reference, were those characteristic of pre-industrial societies ... together with eastern religious models which stressed spiritual awareness, and a certain directness and frankness in social relations which were firmly distinguished from the desire for material improvement. Under the impact of these and other changes, a unilinear modernisation theory became impossible to sustain.

(Robin Cohen, The Sociology of Development and the Development of Sociology, *Social Science Teacher*, **12**, no. 2, 1982, pp. 52–57.)

An interest in Eastern religion, perhaps in the 'Zen way' (remember the quote from Sahlins in chapter 2), the report of the Club of Rome, *The Limits to Growth* (D. H. Meadows et al., Earth Island Ltd, London, 1972), the oil crisis of 1973, the defeat of the USA by a nation of peasants, all these factors formed a background in the 1960s and 1970s to a general re-evaluation of life in advanced industrial society. This was critical of 'materialism' and the 'rat race'. The ideas of Illich (see chapter 7) are a product of this time. While there was most interest in these ideas among the affluent of the First World, they struck few chords with those in the Third World whose problems were of an altogether different kind, beyond the inclusion of a few 'ecological' paragraphs in development plans aimed at liberal foreign advisers.

One outcome of this critical ferment was the growth of the ecology movement, now known as the Green Movement. Many of their critical comments about industrial society are appealing, and may indeed cause us to think about nuclear power, recycling resources, healthier diet and lifestyle in general. Insofar as demand for cheap minerals and other natural resources is part of the problem that the rich world makes for the poor, these ideas do have implications for the Third World. But the Green Movement also has other implications. Intermediate, or appropriate, technology, non-capital intensive but innovative agricultural methods, appreciation of the value and developmental possibilities of Third World medical, cultural and agricultural practice, all these areas now receive serious attention in development debates. Twenty years ago they would not have done. But, bearing in mind my remarks in chapter 2 about the danger of 'utopias', we should not be too ready to dismiss all the technical and material benefits of industrialisation and 'modernity'. The Third World has changed, is changing and will continue to change. The best future that 'development' may offer is probably some combination of 'rediscovered', but appropriate 'traditional' practices, ideas and technology with some of the technology, culture and ideas of the First World. But, as sociologists we must remember that this can happen only if people make it happen. And they can only do this if they have the social power to protect their long term interests (see box 9.6).

Box 9.6 *Soil erosion, conservation and society*

This extract is from a book by a geographer. He sets the problem of soil erosion and land-use within a social and political context.

'. . . practical projects, even on a small scale, must be used to change people's minds about how they relate to each other and the environment. Social forestry in the strict sense of the word (forestry for local ends, benefiting local society), technology for small peasants such as agro-silviculture, small cooperative ventures in soil conserving land use and erosion works, rascal-proof systems for local control of watersheds, forest land, fuel-wood lots, water resources and such like . . . can be used to demonstrate the vital link between the democratic control by all local land-users of their environment and successful conservation. These are the kinds of project which are very slow to show results. . . . Frequently they stand a better chance the less they have to do with central government. Local peasant organisations, rural trade unions, women's groups and other often fragmented and politically fragile institutions can be encouraged and financed by voluntary or non-governmental organisations, but small, fund-starved schemes have to withstand constant pressure from central government and local vested interests. . . . They cannot hope to become the 'answer'

to conservation since they run counter to all the powerful interests discussed in this book ... (but) ... States, governments
and bureaucracies are never monolithic. There are struggles
for power, conflicts of interest ... in the intersticies of government, a soil conservationist can still successfully pursue policies
which may run counter to most interests of persons in government and in official politics.'

(Blaikie, P. M., *The Political Economy of Soil Erosion*, Longman, Harlow, 1985,
pp. 155–156.)

Summary

In this chapter, we have seen that 'development' cannot be
easily defined or measured. It is, after all, a potently political
and emotive term. As sociologists, perhaps we should follow
Weber's advice as to method. He said that sociology should
attempt to understand the rational meaning of social situations
for the actors. On this advice, we can see that 'development'
will inevitably mean very different things for different individuals and social groups. Sociology can tell us a little of the
social reasons why people believe that which they believe about
development; how they try to impose those beliefs on others,
and how it might be possible for the powerless both to express
and to achieve their visions for a better life.

10

Case material

We have seen that the labour migrant with whom the book began was not setting off alone on the journey to town. Labour migrants, peasants, women, industrial workers, schoolchildren – all are actors in the great social changes which are occurring in the Third World. At times they may seem powerless in the face of these changes. But they are all involved, in a multiplicity of groups, as individuals, as producers and consumers, as refugees and guerilla fighters, as poets and as musicians, through culture and through labour, in the construction of *their* development and *their* future. Inevitably, their development and their future is also our own, for the world has, in the past five hundred years, become one system of political, economic and cultural relations.

In this chapter I am going to review some of the topics mentioned in earlier chapters, looking at different aspects, as well as introducing some fresh material. A selection of readings, linked by some comments and questions, should help you to think more deeply about some of the issues. I have chosen these readings in order to provide both some 'hard' statistical information and some 'flavour' of the Third World. We begin with some basic geography.

Where is the Third World?

The map opposite has been marked with national boundaries. Each country has a number. Using the list of countries in chapter 2 (pages 33–34) as a starting point, try to identify the country which goes with each number. Then answer the questions at the top of page 194.

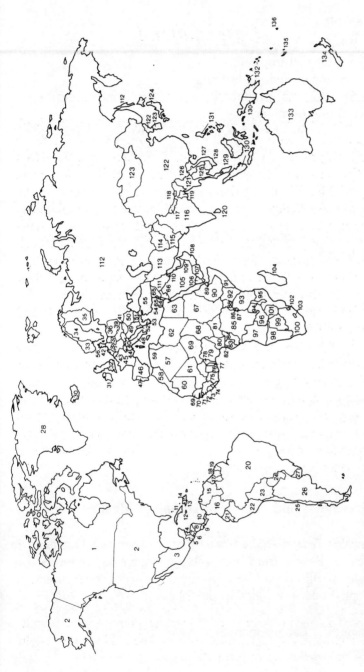

Figure 1 *Where is the Third World?*

Questions

1. What do these countries have in common?
2. Are they all tropical?
3. Are any of them industrialised?
4. Are they all producers of primary commodities, either agricultural or mineral?
5. The list in chapter 9 (page 173) gives some descriptions which have been used for the Third World. How adequate is each of the labels for describing each of the countries you have identified?

Sectoral Distribution of GDP for Selected Countries, 1960 and 1979

The bar chart on page 195 shows the changes in the contribution of various types of economic activity to GDP in a number of countries.

Questions

1. Which countries could you say had undergone some development?
2. What criteria are you using to describe 'development'?
3. Is Britain now more- or less-developed since its industrial sector has declined?

Households and Labour Migration in Mexico

Lourdes Arizpe studied two villages, Toxi and Dotejiare, in Mexico. People from both villages migrate as labourers. But there are differences between the two villages and between the people in each of them, as the following extracts show.

Reading 1 Labour migration in Mexico

'Unemployment and out-migration are differentially correlated

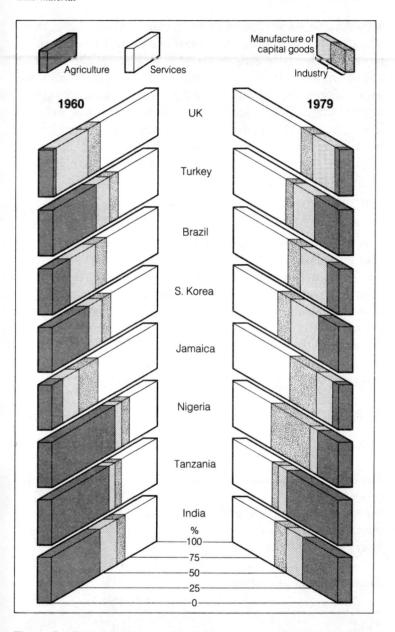

Figure 2 *Sectoral distribution of GDP for selected countries, 1960 and 1979*
(Source: *Third World Atlas*, Crow, B. and Thomas, A., Open University Press, Milton
Keynes, 1983, p. 18.)

according to social classes in rural communities. Agricultural labourers feel the impact of fluctuations in their labour market more directly and are more prone to migrate as the result of unemployment. At the other end, wealthy peasants can fall back on their own resources so that their sons and daughters migrate primarily in search of educational and social mobility. The causes of migration are far more complex for the largest rural group, that of the small landholding peasants. They migrate in response to rural unemployment, or else to contribute to the household income or to attain social mobility. . . .' (p. 20)

'According to the national census of 1970, both Toxi and Dotejiare are considered peasant communities, since 67 and 88 per cent respectively of the fathers of the families work in agriculture. If we only look at the father's occupation the result of our household survey in the villages coincides with the census, as shown in table I. However, the survey results also show that a majority of the fathers engage not only in agricultural work, *but combine it with some other activity*.' (pp. 27–28)

Table I *Distribution of main occupations of fathers*

Occupation	Toxi	Dotejiare
Agriculture only	25%	10%
	(16)	(6)
Agriculture and extractive activities:	27%	85%
(*pulque* or *zacatón*)	(17)	(52)
Subsistence agriculture and	30%	0
migratory wage labour	(19)	–
Local wage labour only	11%	2%
	(7)	(1)
Migratory wage labour only	6%	2%
	(4)	(1)
Total	100%	100%
	(63)	(60)

'According to the [census], 82 per cent of the cases in Toxi and 95 per cent of those in Dotejiare are involved in agriculture, which would lead to the conclusion that these communities are primarily peasant economies. But we arrive at a different conclusion if the activities of the *entire household* labour force are analysed ... taking into account all the working adults, both men and women.'

'Table II shows the distortion that results from classifying the household as a peasant one, on the basis of the father's occupation alone. It becomes clear that wage labour is the predominant occupation in Toxi. In Dotejiare ... now only twelve per cent of the population is dependent on a wage. Toxi, then, in spite of the appearances, is no longer a peasant community.' (pp. 28–29)

Table II *Main occupation of all household workers*

	Agriculture	Unpaid domestic labour	Wage	Total
Toxi	21%	32%	47%	100%
	(45)	(69)	(100)	(214)
Dotejiare	53%	35%	12%	100%
	(107)	(70)	(25)	(202)

'By examining the distribution of labour within the households we can evaluate both their capacity to absorb labour and their need for cash income from wage labour. In Toxi, 53 per cent of the households have one or more members who work in agriculture; in Dotejiare the figure is 96 per cent. Of those, in Dotejiare 54 per cent have a single agricultural worker, 32 per cent have two and the remaining families have three. The latter include two families with medium sized land holdings and seven that are large landowners. In these cases, the sons do not actually work as farm labourers, but oversee hired help or tend the family store. This is in marked contrast to Toxi, where 92 per cent of the households employing agricultural workers have only one such labourer and eight per cent have three. . . .' (p. 29)

'. . . The figures suggest that in most households in both villages there is only enough work in the family fields to occupy a single full-time worker. In Dotejiare the processing of zacatan (a saleable grass) and the making of pulque (an alcoholic beverage derived from a cactus) allows for a second full-time worker in one third of the households. However, the crops require intensive labour . . . (which) . . . is provided by family members who migrate temporarily, and by unpaid female domestic workers. . . .' (p. 29)

'. . . In 90 per cent of the cases in both villages, households include unpaid female domestic workers. The remaining 10 per cent are special cases of widows. How many female workers work within the household? In 80 per cent of the cases in Dotejiare, and 94 per cent in Toxi, there is only one such worker. This indicates that a large number of elder daughters who would otherwise appear in our survey, have left their homes. . . .' (p. 30)

'Wage labourers were present in 89 per cent of Toxi households and 28 per cent of the households in Dotejiare; of those in Toxi 59 per cent had one worker, 30 per cent had two and the remaining 11 per cent had three. In Dotejiare 81 per cent had one wage labourer and the remaining 19 per cent had two. This contrast is very significant; it shows the need for multiple cash incomes in Toxi.'

'But it becomes even more revealing if we analyse where they work and in what type of wage employment. Table III [opposite] confirms the disappearance of sources of wage employment in the areas that have not been replaced by new ones.' (p. 30)

'We know that in Toxi the majority of the migrants are men, while in Dotejiare almost all are women. But what position do these migrants occupy within the household? In Dotejiare, there is no correlation between position within the household and migration, whereas in Toxi a clear pattern emerges; first the

Table III   *Percentage of local and migratory wage labour*

	Local	Migratory	Total
Toxi	14%	86%	47%
	(14)	(86)	(100)
Dotejiare	20%	80%	12%
	(5)	(20)	(25)

father migrates, and then, progressively, as the sons and daughters grow up, each migrates in turn. I have called this pattern *relay migration.*'

'This type of migration is a response to specific needs of households during the domestic cycle. For Toxi families, the critical stages in terms of the balance between workers and dependents begins around the time the mother is twenty five, and persists until she has reached the age of forty five. During these twenty five years at least one cash income, and sometimes several, are ensured by the wage labour of some members of the family. To achieve this, at least three or four children are necessary if the father is to be substituted in the migration ... in order to provide the wage income required over a period of twenty years, we can estimate that the family needs three sons or a combination of four sons and daughters.' (p. 31)

(Arizpe, L., Relay Migration and the Survival of the Peasant Household, in Safa, H. I. (ed.), *Towards a Political Economy of Urbanisation in Third World Countries*, Oxford University Press, New Delhi, 1982, pp. 20–30.)

Questions

1. Why might the people of Toxi be unwilling to adopt family planning?
2. How, and in what ways, is this system of labour migration dependent on female work?
3. In the light of this extract, how useful is it to distinguish between 'urban' and 'rural' society?

4. Why do you think these people migrate? Why don't they stay in the city?

5. What does the phrase the 'family needs three sons or four sons and a daughter' tell us about the viewpoint of the writer? Gender bias?

Social Evolution and Conservatism: America

In chapter 1 we saw how influential evolutionary theory has been in sociological theory. We also saw that 'theory' and 'ideology' can shade into each other. In this reading, Hofstadter tells us something of why social evolutionism was so well received in the USA.

Reading 2   Social evolutionism in the USA

'The subject of this book is the effect of Darwin's work upon social thinking in America. In some respects the United States during the last three decades of the nineteenth century and at the beginning of the twentieth century was *the* Darwinian country. England gave Darwin to the world, but the United States gave to Darwinism an unusually quick and sympathetic reception . . . Herbert Spencer, who of all men made the most ambitious attempt to systematise the implication of evolution in fields other than biology itself, was far more popular in the United States than he was in his native country.

An age of rapid and striking economic change, the age during which Darwin's and Spencer's ideas were popularised in the United States was also one in which the prevailing political mood was conservative. . . .

Understandably Darwinism was seized upon as a welcome addition, perhaps the most powerful of all, to the store of ideas to which solid and conservative men appealed when they wished to reconcile their fellows to some of the hardships of life and to prevail upon them not to support hasty and ill-considered reforms. Darwinism was one of the great informing insights in this long phase in the history of the conservative mind in America. It was those who wished to defend the political status quo, above all the laissez-faire conservatives, who were first to pick up the instruments of social argument that were forged out of the Darwinian concepts. . . .

Darwinism was used to buttress the conservative outlook in two ways. The most popular catchwords of Darwinism, "struggle for existence" and "survival of the fittest", when applied to the life of man in society, suggested that nature would provide that the best competitors in a competitive situation would win, and that this process would lead to continuing improvement. In itself this was not a new idea . . . but it did give the force of natural law to the idea of competitive struggle. Secondly, the idea of development over aeons brought new force to another familiar idea in conservative political theory, the conception that all sound development must be slow and unhurried. Society should be envisaged as an organism . . . which could change only at the glacial pace at which new species are produced in nature . . . the conclusions to which Darwinism was at first put were conservative conclusions. They suggested that all attempts to reform social processes were efforts to remedy the irremedi-able, that they interfered with the wisdom of nature, that they could only lead to degeneration.'

(Hofstadter, R., *Social Darwinism in American Thought*, Beacon Press, Boston, 1959 [first published 1944], pp. 4–7.)

Questions

1. Why do you think that Darwinism received 'an unusually quick and sympathetic reception' in America? What period of American history is Hofstadter writing about?
2. How does Darwinism 'defend the political status quo'?
3. In what two ways was Darwinism used to 'buttress the conservative outlook'?
4. What does the phrase 'the wisdom of nature' mean?

Manufacturing and Development

Warren, arguing against the pessimism of dependency theorists, suggests that capitalist development is occurring in the Third World. In supporting this view, he suggests that the share of manufacturing in GDP indicates that there is more 'development' than Frank and others would have us believe.

Reading 3 The share of manufacture in GDP

'If the advance of modern manufacturing is crucial to the elimination of underdevelopment, then the proportion of gross domestic product in the underdeveloped countries accounted for by manufacturing is a useful, if only approxiate comparative indicator. The figures are rather impressive. For the LDCs as a whole, manufacturing accounted for 14.5 per cent of gross domestic production 1950–4; the figure rose to 17.9 per cent in 1960 and 20.4 per cent in 1973. In the developed capitalist countries manufacturing contributed 28.4 per cent to GDP in 1973. *The difference is therefore becoming rather small.*

Aggregate figures, however, can be misleading if we are concerned with the rise of alternative centres of economic power in the Third World rather than with overall changes. Indeed, the very concept of a Third World separated by a gap from the developed world as a whole implies a polarity that is not always real. [The table opposite] shows quite clearly that in a number of large and medium-sized underdeveloped economies (in addition to some small ones, like Hong Kong and Malta) manufacturing already makes a contribution to gross domestic product comparable or even superior to that of some of the developed capitalist economies. In Mexico, Argentina, Chile, Brazil, Korea and Taiwan, for example, manufacturing accounts for a proportion of GDP similar to that in the developed market economies as a whole; indeed, in some of these countries it contributes more to gross domestic product than it does in Canada, Denmark, Australia, Norway, Sweden, Finland, New Zealand and the United States.

A number of other countries are also approaching the position

of the developed capitalist economies in this respect. Costa
Rica, Uruguay, and Peru now fall in the same range as Canada,
New Zealand, Spain, Norway, Finland and Australia.'

*Selected countries' manufacturing as a percentage of Gross Domestic
Product . . . (1973) and percentage of active labour force employed
in manufacturing (latest estimates)*

Country	Manufacturing as % of GDP	% of active labour force employed in manufacturing
Egypt	21.6	12.9
Taiwan	29.8	n.a.
South Korea	24.3	20.5
Argentina	38.3	19.7
Brazil	24.6	11.0
Chile	25.9	15.9
Costa Rica	21.9	11.9
Mexico	25.4	17.8
Peru	21.4	12.5
Uruguay	23.0	18.8
average	25.6	*average* 15.7
Australia	26.6	24.8
Canada	20.1	18.0
Denmark	26.6	23.1
Norway	25.4	24.4
Sweden	24.8	26.5
United States	24.7	22.4
average	24.7	*average* 23.2
Greece	20.4	17.1
Spain	26.7	25.7
Malta	26.5	27.8
Hong Kong	32.1	44.4
Singapore	26.1	25.6

(Warren, B., 1980, pp. 244–245.)

Questions

1. What does Warren mean when he says that 'the gross proportion of gross domestic product ... accounted for by manufacturing is a useful, if only approximate, comparative indicator'? Why is it only approximate?
2. Why can aggregate figures, such as those in the table, be misleading?
3. What other indicators of the 'elimination of underdevelopment' might you use instead?
4. Why do you think that Warren uses the term LDCs (less developed countries) rather than 'underdeveloped countries' (see chapter 2)?

Per Capita Income and Underdevelopment

In contrast to Warren, Walter Rodney, a Guyanan who taught for some years at the university in Tanzania, argues that the real division is between 'developed' and 'underdeveloped' countries, and that differences in per capita income clearly divide the world into these two groups.

Reading 4 The gap between Africa and the developed countries

'[The table opposite] gives a clear picture of the gap between Africa and certain nations measured in per capita incomes. It is the gap that allows one group to be called "developed" and another "underdeveloped"....

The gap ... is not only great, but is also increasing. All of the countries named as "underdeveloped" in the world are exploited by others; and the underdevelopment with which the world is now pre-occupied is a product of capitalist, imperialist and colonialist exploitation. African and Asian societies were developing independently until they were taken over directly or indirectly by the capitalist powers. When that happened,

Countries	Per capita income in $US (1968)	
Canada	2,247	
USA	3,578	
France	1,738	(1967)
United Kingdom	1,560	(1967)
AFRICA as a whole	140	(1965)
Congo	52	
Ghana	198	
Kenya	107	
Malawi	52	
Morocco	185	
South Africa	543	
Tanzania	62	
United Arab Republic	156	
Zambia	226	

exploitation increased and *the export of surplus ensued,* depriving the societies of the benefit of their natural resources and labour. That is an integral part of underdevelopment in the contemporary sense.'

(Rodney, W., *How Europe Underdeveloped Africa*, Bougle-L'Ouverture Publications, 1976, pp. 22–24.)

Questions

1. Does the information in the table allow one group of countries to be called 'developed' and the other 'underdeveloped'?
2. How does Rodney's approach differ theoretically from that of Warren? (You might want to look at chapter 2 to help you in answering this question.)
3. How do Rodney and Warren differ in their views of the impact of capitalism and imperialism on the Third World?

Urbanisation

The accompanying table (taken from World Development Report, IBRD, Washington, 1985) gives you some information about rates of urbanisation in a number of Third World, as well as some developed, countries.

Country	Urban population				Percentage of urban population					
	as % of total pop.		average annual growth rate (%)		in largest city		in cities >500,000 persons		no. of cities >500,000 persons	
	1965	1983	1965–73	1973–83	1960	1980	1960	1980	1960	1980
Ethiopia	8	15	7.4	6.0	30	37	0	37	0	1
Zaire	19	38	5.9	6.9	14	28	14	38	1	2
Tanzania	6	14	8.1	8.6	34	50	0	50	0	1
India	18	24	4.0	4.2	7	6	26	39	11	36
Benin	11	16	4.5	4.7	–	63	0	63	0	1
China	18	21	–	–	6	6	42	45	38	78
Ghana	26	38	4.5	5.3	25	35	0	48	0	2
Kenya	9	17	7.3	8.0	40	57	0	57	0	1
Senegal	27	34	4.3	3.8	53	65	0	65	0	1
Bolivia	26	43	8.9	3.3	47	44	0	44	0	1
Indonesia	16	24	4.1	4.8	20	23	34	50	3	9
Egypt	41	45	3.0	2.9	38	39	53	53	2	2
Morocco	32	43	4.0	4.2	16	26	16	50	1	4
Peru	52	67	4.7	3.6	38	39	38	44	1	2
Korea	32	62	6.5	4.8	35	41	61	77	3	7
UK	87	91	0.7	0.3	24	20	61	55	15	17
France	67	80	2.0	1.2	25	23	34	34	4	6
Japan	67	76	2.4	1.3	18	22	35	42	5	9
USA	72	74	1.6	1.2	13	12	61	77	40	65
USSR	52	65	5.9	–3.4	6	4	21	33	25	50

Questions

1. How might you account for the rapid increase in urban population in Korea between 1965 and 1983?
2. Why do you think that urban population has decreased in the United States?

3. Do you think that, overall, this table provides evidence of 'development'? Can you assume that the same processes are at work in all of these countries? For example, is increased urbanisation in Korea likely to be for the same reasons as in Ethiopia?

4. How could you explain the fact that between 1965 and 1983 urban population in China rose from 18 to 21 per cent, while the number of cities with populations over 500,000 increased from 38 to 78 between 1960 and 1980?

Peasants and Innovation: India

In the 1960s, Michael Lipton studied Kavathe village in India. He was trying to discover why Indian farmers persisted in their old practices when there were apparently more efficient and profitable ways to cultivate the land. He argues that, far from being 'irrational' or 'conservative', their behaviour was rational. He is following Weber's suggestion that we must try to understand social behaviour from the participant's perspective.

Reading 5   Farmers' decisions in Kavathe

'... almost every farmer in Kavathe has discovered a set of rules to ensure survival: what I call a survival algorithm. That is, he has found a group of practices, a group of decisions, which allows him to muddle through in good years and bad alike. Naturally he is reluctant to change it.

Can this explain the ... sorts of behaviour which led us to question profit-maximizing explanations in Kavathe? The acceptance of apparently irrational constraints is a social survival mechanism for the village as a whole. Many of these constraints stem from the caste system, even when they are not directly enjoined by it. Caste provides a social ordering within the village; if sons do the same jobs as their fathers this cuts down the squabbling that would be linked to the job competition in a poor and status-conscious society. The caste system is not entirely inflexible. Any casteman may earn more money as a skilful farmer. But caste does provide order – and divides big villages into groups of castemen, small and loyal enough to help each other in emergency. . . . At present, even low-caste villagers accept the caste system as a least evil – part of a communal survival algorithm that is known to work, however badly.

Fear of disrupting this algorithm also explains why all villagers are reluctant to adopt some farming innovations. Just as the American businessman fights harder to raise his market share when it has been falling, so the Indian villager needs a big incentive to take risks with allegedly improved practices, so long as the old practices he knows and trusts do not lead to an actual fall in living standards – and they have not.'

(Lipton, M., Game Against Nature: Theories of Peasant Decision-making, in Harriss, J. C. (ed.), 1982, pp. 266–267.)

Questions

1. What does Lipton mean by a 'survival algorithm'? Can you think of examples of your survival algorithm?
2. Lipton wrote this before the Green Revolution became widespread in India. What effect do you think the Green Revolution might have had on the survival algorithm of a small, nearly landless farmer in Kavathe (see chapter 6).
3. Why are small farmers in India unlikely to be profit-maximisers?

Peasant Differentiation and the State: The Gambia

Margaret Haswell first studied the village of Genieri in The Gambia in 1947. She returned in 1973. In this extract she describes some of the changes which had occurred in the intervening years.

Reading 6   Social change in Genieri

'Any movement from one stage of economic development to another requires not only a catalyst, but also a large reserve of human energy to enable communities to take advantage of it. Failure at the community level caused by agencies mainly outside its control has provided opportunities for gain to those few individuals whose resource endowment has been particularly favourable under the prevailing environmental conditions. In the late forties social status favoured those who could claim to be direct descendants of the original settlers; the village headman was in legal theory regarded as having control over village land, but it was the compound head who exercised greatest control; and the local assessment of land value was measured as work – work necessary to clear the land and work involved in production.

Today power is vested in those who are the salaried servants of government and who can bring authority to bear on "erring" individuals . . . and in the private sector power is represented by the merchant and the moneylender. . . .

Realignments which are seen to have taken place over a generation in the power structure and level of living of this rural community strongly suggest that external factors have become so severe as to make it generally impossible for farming to finance itself from within family reserves.

It is the collusion between the petty bureaucrats and the small-time businessman that has largely kept the common man subsistence-tied. . . .'

(Haswell, M., *The Nature of Poverty*, Macmillan, 1975, pp. 184–185.)

Questions

1. What does Haswell mean by 'agencies mainly outside its control'?
2. What are the main changes in the source of community

power which have occurred in the time since Haswell first studied this community?

3. How was land value assessed forty years ago?

Women and Land Tenure Reform: Kenya

In Kenya as in many countries, attempts have been made to change land tenure arrangements. Sometimes, as in this case, these have involved the registration of ownership in the names of individuals. This replaces traditional tenure systems where land was available to those who worked it, and where 'ownership', in the sense of being able to buy and sell land, was unknown. In these traditional systems women, as the main producers, usually have protected rights to land. Registration is undertaken so that farmers can use land as security for loans from government and banks with a view to improving and expanding their farming. Achola Pala Okeyo studied the impact of such a policy on Luo women.

Reading 7 Land registration in Kenya

'Data from a study conducted by the author in 1974–75 . . . describe a typical situation of Luo women with respect to land rights in the tenure reform. A portion of the field research surveyed 135 in-marrying females . . . on the current position of women regarding land tenure. We were interested in the following issues: women's access rights to land; how they acquired the land they are currently using; how they use the land; who holds the right of allocation of the land they are farming; the status of women's cultivation rights in relation to men's allocative rights; whether some or all of the land they are using has been bought or sold recently; whether their land is being registered, and, if so, in whose name; and how decisions are made regarding the sale, use, or exchange of land.

In response to the first question concerning the amount of land over which respondents have cultivation rights, 23.0 percent said they have access to at least one parcel and not more than three parcels; 46.0 percent reported access to between three and five parcels; and 23.0 percent said they had access to between six and nine parcels. . . . Five respondents said they were landless.

From this, it can be concluded that 91.9 percent of the respondents have access to land ranging between 1.5 and 4.5 hectares. Only two respondents (1.5 percent) have land between 5.7 and 7.5 hectares. Furthermore, only these latter two respondents reported that their land is consolidated all around their homestead. . . . This means that none of the respondents have enough land to qualify for the agricultural loan scheme meant for small farmers in Kenya. . . .

It seemed important . . . to enquire how far the process of land registration had been implemented and whose names were actually being entered in the land register. . . .

To the question of land registration, 97.0 percent said that their land is already registered. When asked in whose name the land is registered and their own relationship to the registered owner, 51.9 percent said that their land is registered in their husband's name; 25.9 percent reported the registered owner to be their son; 7.4 percent said that their land is registered in the joint names of their husband and son; 6.0 percent reported joint registration in their name and their son's name; and only 5.9 percent reported that land is registered in their own names.

The striking point in these results is the manner in which land is being transferred to an almost exclusively male, individualised tenure-system which leaves no provision concerning how women's access rights are to be defined when the reform is completed and the new tenure system becomes operational. Of all the respondents, 85.2 percent reported that their land is already registered in the name of their husband, son, or jointly in the husband's and son's names. If we add to this those respondents who have land registered jointly in their own name and their son's name . . . we find that 91.1 percent are eventually to depend on land whose registered owner is a male relative.'

(Okeyo, A. P., Daughters of the Lakes and Rivers: Colonization and Rights of Luo Women, in Etienne, M. and Leacock, E. (eds.) *Women and Colonisation: Anthropological Approaches*, Praegar, New York, 1980, pp. 203–206.)

Questions

1. Why does the government want to register land?
2. Why are women unlikely to obtain government grants and loans as frequently as men?
3. What long term effects might this policy have on the production of subsistence crops?

Urban Working Women: China

When the Chinese Communist Party took power in 1949, one of its socialist policies was to improve the position of women. Elizabeth Croll has studied the position of women in China over a number of years. She concludes that their position has improved enormously since before the revolution. This does not mean, though, that gender discrimination has disappeared.

Reading 8   Urban women in China

'In the cities and towns of China there are very few women not employed full-time in the waged-labour force. In 1979 it was estimated that only about 10% of urban women were not in employment and these were mainly the elderly and retired, the weak, the disabled and those who were awaiting job assignment. Working women are to be found in a wide range of occupations including the professions, skilled and unskilled factory work and service industries. They are well represented in the professions from medicine and engineering to teaching, and this has not led to a downgrading of these professions in the occupational hierarchy as in some parts of Eastern Europe. This is probably because of the continuing scarcity of such professional skills in a country as large and as poor as China still is. However, the sexual division of labour in urban employment is still based on the premise that women are more suited for work in certain industries than others. Generally they are not thought to be capable of heavy physical labour because of their physiological characteristics, and accordingly women make up only a small proportion, some 15% of the work force, in some heavy industries. On the other hand, women are thought to be "particularly dexterous, attentive and patient". On this basis, textiles, weaving and other light industries and services employ a high proportion of women labourers, on average about 69% more than the heavy industrial sector.'

(Croll, E., *Chinese Women Since Mao*, Zed Press, 1983, p. 43.)

Questions

1. What percentage of urban women were not in employment?
2. What does 'downgrading of these professions' mean?
3. Why do women only make up about 15 per cent of the workforce in heavy industry?

Medicine in the Third World

In this section, we look at two aspects of medical practice in the Third World. The first is the 'brain drain' of doctors and the second is the role of transnationals in the provision of medicines.

Reading 9   The brain drain

'[In the Third World]. . . . Those selected as medical students are invariably members of the urban elite. Already cut off economically, socially and culturally from the mass of the local population, students then undergo a process of western medical socialisation. This turns out doctors with what one writer has described as "the trained incapacity for rural practice which is itself the product of the British system of medical training within large centralised hospitals". Thus, doctors are encouraged to develop intellectual preoccupations in specialised clinical fields. In India, for example, where opportunities for specialisation have expanded rapidly since the 1950s, there are now about one-third as many annual enrolments in postgraduate medicine as in undergraduate training. Moves towards specialisation, however, are probably most advanced in Latin America, where only a minority of doctors work in general practice. While these developments are obviously antithetical to the objective health needs of third world populations, they are strongly defended by doctors, who emphasise the over-riding importance of "intellectual stimulation" and "professional satisfaction". . . .'

'. . . control over medical education by the internationally organised medical profession, in conjunction with the economic command of the market by western countries, has added skilled labour to the flow of resources leaving the third world. The significance of these transfers was illustrated by a recent UNCTAD report which estimated that in 1970 the trained manpower resources transferred to the USA were worth $3,700 million – a figure in excess of the entire US non-military foreign aid budget for the same year. More specifically, it has been suggested that the *annual* loss to Latin America caused by the flow of doctors to the US is equivalent in value to the total volume of medical aid from the US to Latin America during the decade 1960–70. The most obvious consequence of these movements of skilled workers has been the exacerbation of existing international inequalities in the distribution of doctors, nurses and midwives. Thus the long-standing shortage of trained health workers in the third world is perpetuated, while shortages in Britain, West Germany or the USA are filled by men and women trained at the expense of some of the poorest people in the world.'

(Doyal, L., *The Political Economy of Health*, Pluto Press, 1977, pp. 262–264.)

Questions

1. Why has the demand for postgraduate medical education expanded in India?

2. What does the phrase 'objective health needs of third world populations' mean?
3. What is the meaning of 'trained incapacity for rural practice'?
4. What kind of development theory underlies this analysis?

Reading 10 Medicines and transnationals

'The most important – and best documented example – of medicine as a commodity is provided by the multinational pharmaceutical industry. Although overall medical expenditure in the third world is much less than in the developed world, expenditure on drugs is proportionately very much greater. Whereas in Britain, drugs account for about eleven per cent of NHS spending, they represent roughly twenty-five per cent of the health budget in most African countries, and in some third world countries, they absorb as much as forty or fifty per cent of total health expenditure. . . . Even where international corporations have been compelled by law to licence indigenous firms to manufacture a patented drug, the time lag involved in starting local production has often allowed the original producer to develop a new drug to supersede the first. . . . It is important to appreciate, however, that the bulk of drug production in the third world is controlled by multinational corporations and consists simply of the formulating and packaging of imported chemicals. Since these imports normally come from another subsidiary of the same corporation, internal accounting mechanisms are frequently used by firms to inflate the cost of the constituent chemicals, and hence the price of the finished product. This practice – known as transfer pricing – has been well documented in the drug industry, with the most notorious example coming from Colombia, where in 1968 the imported chemical constituent of valium was found to be overpriced by 6,584 per cent.'

(Doyal, L., 1977, pp. 266–267.)

Themes in the Sociology of Development

Questions

1. Why is expenditure on drugs proportionately higher in the Third World than in Britain?
2. What is 'transfer pricing'?

Afterword

I began this book with the image of the labour migrant. I shall end it with a story about a real labour migrant.

In 1977, I spent two months in The Gambia making an assessment of the likely social impact of a scheme to place a barrage across the River Gambia. The intention of the project was to increase the land available for rice cultivation and to improve communications by providing a road bridge from northern Senegal to southern Senegal across the river, while at the same time linking the north and south sides of The Gambia.

During my stay in that country, I had as my assistant and interpreter a young Gambian man. Prior to working for me, he had been unemployed. Indeed, like many other people in the Third World (and in Britain) he had been more or less unemployed since he finished school. He had gone to considerable lengths to find work, including stowing away on a ship to Nigeria, but in that case he had been discovered and sent back home.

We spent a lot of time travelling around The Gambia and stayed in a number of villages. In the evenings, outside our temporary homes, we talked about many things. He was curious to find out about my life and my experience – I was, after all, supposed to be some kind of 'expert' on development. He was coming to his own conclusions about the subject, and in his way was much more of an expert than I was. He was trying very hard to make sense of his life and his society, trying to discover meaning in a world which seemed quite unable to provide him with a basic and secure level of life. When the time came for me to leave for Britain, it was with some sadness, our lives were literally worlds apart, and there was little that I could do to help him.

We corresponded for some months, then there was an interval. About a year later, I received a letter from Nigeria. He had made a lengthy and hazardous journey there (he was robbed on the way), by train and by lorry, and was now barely existing by working illegally as a labourer on a construction site – Nigeria was experiencing an 'oil boom'. He lived thus for some time, always wary of the authorities, until in the end all foreign workers were expelled. Once again, he had to move. This time he went to Libya, and once again found work with a construction company, another 'oil-boom'. This lasted for about a year, and then he was unemployed and had to move on. He travelled to Tunisia, stayed a few months before crossing the Mediterranean to Italy. I don't know how he survived there, but after a period of months, he left and went to Sweden in 1984 where, he says, 'I have been writing poetry and some other things which I came to understand about life by living with different people in West Africa, southern and northern Europe'.

The point of this story is that he is learning from his very hard experiences. He is developing a Third World world-view, and in his own way is making his own history, developing his own perspective on the development process. He is not alone in this. All of the peoples of the Third World, the majority of the world's population, are involved in a struggle to understand, to act on that understanding, and to develop themselves, but always in relation to a world which they did not make, but within whose constraints they are forced to act. It is a world in which the links between the First, Second and Third Worlds are daily becoming more binding on us all.

It is something of the nature of this history-making in the Third World which this book has attempted to elucidate through the study of sociology.

Glossary

The purpose of this glossary is to explain the special meanings of the words printed in bold in the text. These explanations are not intended to be exhaustive, they are meant to enable you to read some of the more difficult parts more easily. There would be no point in learning them as definitions as many of them are the subject of extensive discussion and debate.

For more detailed explanations, you could consult *The Social Science Encyclopaedia* by A. and J. Kuper, or *The Fontana Dictionary of Modern Thought* (Fontana, 1986).

Alienation

Derived from the work of Marx (and others), it describes the experience of people in capitalist society, their feeling that they have no control over their fate, play no part in social life beyond giving obedience to an employer or to the law, and have no control over the products of their labour because these do not belong to them but to the owners of capital.

Anomie

The social condition in which dominant beliefs are questioned or repudiated. As a result, individuals are confused as to correct ways of behaving. Durkheim noted that such a state of affairs could develop in times of either extreme social and economic decline or of prosperity. Related, but different from, the idea of alienation (q.v.).

Articulation

When two or more modes of production (q.v.) come into contact and the people and resources of one enter into the production processes of the other, then articulation is said to occur between them. The case of the Arab merchant in Darfur (p. 102) is a good empirical example of how this might occur.

Differentiation

All societies recognise different categories of people – old, young, men, women, ritually pure, ritually impure. Such distinctions are sometimes called sociological or cultural differentiation, in contrast to differentiation *per se* which describes social differences based on unequal access to the means of production – land, tools, capital.

Evolution

Gradual transformation or change through a series of states. Applied by Comte, Spencer and some other thinkers to the development of social organisation which they considered became more complex as evolution occurred.

Functionalist sociology

The tradition of sociological thought which starts from the assumption that societies can be analysed as though they were integrated organisms. This assumption means that social phenomena are explained in relation to their contribution to the maintenance and reinforcement of the whole.

Gemeinschaft

Tonnies' model of a society said to be based on intense emotional relationships between its members. Its organising principles were said to be cooperation, custom, religion, the family, village and the small-town community. Sometimes translated into English as 'community'. The opposite of *Gesellschaft* (q.v.).

Gesellschaft

Tonnies' model of the typical 'modern' society, characterised by large-scale organisation such as the city or the state, and based on law and convention. The opposite of *Gemeinschaft* (q.v.).

Ideology

Social or political beliefs which serve and further the interests of one group rather than another. Marx uses the term to imply that an ideology 'mystifies' the real nature of social inequality so as to defuse social conflict. Hence, religion is 'the opiate' of the people because it may say that the poor will get their reward in heaven. Closely related to the process of legitimation (see legitimate).

Legitimate

Used as a verb to describe how a set of ideas, an ideology (q.v.), defends and maintains the existing position of some dominant social group. A legitimating ideology is one which furthers the belief that the holders of power have the right to exercise that power, that they have authority.

Meaning

Used by Max Weber to describe the understanding a person has of why they are doing something. He uses the example of a person chopping down a tree with an axe, and notes that there could be various meanings of this action for that person. They could believe the tree to be a threatening spirit or they could be collecting firewood. Social behaviours may have all kinds of meanings other than their apparent ones. Think, for example, of somebody answering the telephone in their 'telephone voice'. In one respect they are merely answering the 'phone, in another they are trying to impress somebody.

Mode of production

Derived from the ideas of Marx and Engels, a term which defines types of society in terms of their different property relations. Thus, capitalism is a mode of production based on private property, feudalism is based on property held in the form of a fief, in which the immediate controller of landed property holds it at the will of the person above them in the feudal hierarchy. There may be many different modes of production. In the context of development, an important problem is how they come to be articulated (see articulation).

Patriarchy

Societies in which power is unequally distributed between men and women, and where men always form the dominant group, and women the dominated.

Peasant

A member of a rural social category which is no longer self-sufficient, but has obligations to the state in the form of paying taxes or producing certain crops for sale. In discussions of development issues, this term is often used to describe rural producers whose mode of production (q.v.) has undergone articulation (q.v.) with capitalism.

Peasantisation

The process of becoming a peasant (q.v.). There may be many intermediate stages between being an independent rural producer and being a peasant; hence there are 'mixed forms' such as the semi-independent rural producers who also work for a few weeks in each year as wage labourers (see pp. 119–20).

Positivism

An approach to science which emphasises the importance of empirical observation and verification and tends, if carried to an extreme, to devalue the importance of theoretical and imaginative thought.

Proletarianisation

The processes of becoming members of a working class by which people lose control of the tools and/or land by means of which they have traditionally subsisted. It also refers to the related process in which people cease to be bound by traditional, non-market rules of behaviour such as relations of social or cultural obligation.

Relative deprivation

The idea that people experience poverty or deprivation not only in absolute terms (e.g. starvation) but mainly in relative terms, by comparing their situation to that of others whom they consider significant.

Social solidarity

The term used by Emile Durkheim to describe social cohesion. He distinguished two types, mechanical solidarity, found in 'primitive' societies, and based on similarity between its members, and organic solidarity, found in 'modern' societies, and based on differences mediated through various forms of social institution, such as trades unions and political parties.

Structural transformation

This term describes the transformation of a whole society from being predominantly agricultural and rural to being industrial and urban.

Utopianism

A form of social theory which tries to promote certain desired values and practices by presenting them as part of an ideal, harmonious society. In sociology, it is used to describe theories which present an unrealistic model of society by assuming that conflict is either not present or can be easily resolved.

Value judgement

A statement which makes a judgement as to the rightness or wrongness of some action or state of affairs. It is usually contrasted with a value-free statement, said by some to be characteristic of scientific thought. Value judgements are dangerous when they are not made explicit, but are disguised by introductory words such as 'It is obvious that. . . .'

Bibliography

Abdalla, I-S., Que es el Tercer Mundo, in *Guia del Tercer Mundo* (Mexico: Periodistas del Tercer Mundo 1981).

Amin, S., *Uneven Development* (Harvester Press 1976).

Archer, J. and Lloyd, B., *Sex and Gender* (Penguin Books 1982).

Bacdayan, A. S., Mechanistic Cooperation and Sexual Equality Among the Western Bontoc, in Schlegel, A. (ed.), *Sexual Stratification: a cross-cultural view* (New York: Columbia University 1977).

Barrett, M., *Women's Oppression Today* (Verso Editions 1984).

Barnett, T., *The Gezira Scheme: an illustion of development* (Frank Cass and Co. 1977).

Bellah, R., *Tokugawa Religion: the values of preindustrial Japan* (Glencoe: Free Press 1957).

Bendix, R., *Max Weber: an intellectual portrait* (Methuen 1962).

Bernstein, H., Corrigan, P. and Thorpe, M., *Developed or Being Developed?* (Open University Press 1983).

Black, C. E., *The Dynamics of Modernisation* (New York: Harper and Row 1966).

Blaikie, P. M., *The Political Economy of Soil Erosion* (Longman 1985).

Boserup, E., *Woman's Role in Economic Development* (George Allen and Unwin 1970).

Brandt, W., *North–South: a Programme for Survival* (Pan Books 1983).

Braudel, F., *The Structures of Everyday Life* (William Collins and Sons 1981).

Byres, T. and Crow, B. with Mae Wan Ho, *The Green Revolution in India* (Open University Press 1983).

Castells, E., *The Urban Question: a Marxist approach* (Edward Arnold 1977).

Cohen, R., The Sociology of Development and the Development of Sociology, *Social Science Teacher*, **12**, no. 2, 1983.

Cole, G. D. H. and Filson, A. W., *The British Working Class Movement: selected documents 1789–1875* (New York: St. Martin's Press 1967).

Chodak, S., *Societal Development: five approaches with conclusions from comparative analysis* (New York: Oxford University Press 1973).

Croll, E., *Chinese Women Since Mao* (Zed Press 1983).

Crow, B. and Thomas, A., with Jenkins, R. and Kimble, J., *Third World Atlas* (Open University Press 1983).

225

Dahrendorf, R., *Essays in the Theory of Society* (Routledge and Kegan Paul 1968).

Dinham, B. and Hines, C., *Agribusiness in Africa* (Earth Resources Ltd 1983).

Djilas, M., *The New Class* (Thames and Hudson 1957).

Dore, R., *The Diploma Disease* (George Allen and Unwin 1976).

Doyal, L., *The Political Economy of Health* (Pluto Press 1977).

Durkheim, E., *The Division of Labour in Society* (Toronto: Collier Macmillan 1965).

Durkheim, E., *The Rules of Sociological Method* (New York: The Free Press 1964).

Edwards, C. B., *The Fragmented World* (Methuen 1985).

Eisenstadt, S. N., *Tradition, Change and Modernity* (New York: John Wiley and Sons 1973).

Engels, F., *The Condition of the Working Class in England* (Basil Blackwell 1958).

Etienne, M. and Leacock, E., *Women and Colonization: anthropological perspectives* (New York: Praeger 1980).

Firth, R. and Yamey, B., *Capital, Savings and Credit in Peasant Societies* (Allen and Unwin 1964).

Firth, R. (ed.), *Themes in Economic Anthropology* (Tavistock 1970).

Fletcher, R., *The Crisis of Industrial Civilisation* (Heinemann 1974).

Fontana Dictionary of Modern Thought, edited by Bullock, A. and Stallybrass, O. (Fontana 1986).

Foster, G., *Traditional Cultures and the Impact of Technological Change* (New York: Harper and Row 1962).

Frank, A. G., *Capitalism and Underdevelopment in Latin America* (Penguin Books 1971).

Freeman, D., *Margaret Mead and Samoa* (Cambridge University Press 1983).

Friedmann, D., *Regional Development Policy* (Boston, MIT 1966).

Gerschenkron, A., *Economic Backwardness in Historical Perspective* (Cambridge, Mass.: Harvard University Press 1962).

Golbourne, H. (ed.), *Politics and State in the Third World* (Macmillan 1979).

Harriss, J. C. (ed.), *Rural Development* (Hutchinson 1982).

Haswell, M., *The Nature of Poverty* (Macmillan 1975).

Hobsbawm, E. J., *Worlds of Labour* (Weidenfeld and Nicolson 1984).

Hofstadter, R., *Social Darwinism in American Thought* (Boston: Beacon Press 1959).

Hoselitz, B. F. and Moore, W. E. (eds.), *Industrialization and Society* (UNESCO-MOUTON 1966).

Humphrey, C., *Karl Marx Collective* (Cambridge and Paris: Cambridge University Press and Editions des Sciences de l'Homme 1983).

Bibliography

Illich, I., *Deschooling Society* (Penguin Books 1975).
International Bank for Reconstruction and Development, *The World Development Report 1983* (Washington: IBRD 1983).
International Bank for Reconstruction and Development, *The World Development Report 1985* (Washington: IBRD 1985).

Kerr, K., Dunlop, J. and Harbin, F., *Industrialism and Industrial Man* (Heinemann 1960).
The Koran, translated by N. J. Dawood (Penguin Books 1968).
Kuper, A. and J., *The Social Science Encyclopaedia* (Routledge and Kegan Paul 1985).

Leghorn, L. and Parker, K., *Women's Worth* (Routledge and Kegan Paul 1981).
Lewis, O., *La Vida* (Secker and Warburg 1967).
Levy, M. J., *Modernization and the Structures of Society* (Princeton: Princeton University Press 1966).
Long, N., *Social Change and the Individual: a study of the social and religious responses to innovation* (Manchester University Press 1968).

Malinowski, B., *Coral Gardens and their Magic* (George Allen and Unwin 1922).
Malinowski, B., *Argonauts of the Western Pacific* (Routledge and Kegan Paul 1961).
Mao Tse-tung, *On Kruschev's Phoney Communism and its Historical Lessons for the World* (Peking: Foreign Languages Press n.d.).
Mayer, P. (ed.), *Black Villagers in an Industrial Society* (Capetown: Oxford University Press 1980).
Meadows, D. H., *The Limits to Growth* (Earth Island Ltd. 1972).
Midgley, M., *The Origins of the Specious, New Statesman*, 22 November 1985.
Milliband, R., *The State in Capitalist Society* (Weidenfeld and Nicolson 1969).
Moore, W. E., *Social Change* (New Jersey: Prentice Hall 1964).
Moore, B., *The Social Origins of Dictatorship and Democracy: lord and peasant in the making of the modern world* (Penguin Books 1966).
Morris, M. D., *Measuring the Conditions of the World's Poor* (Pergamon Press 1979).

Nyerere, J. K., *Dar-es-Salaam Daily News*, 21 May 1971.
Nyerere, J. K., *Freedom and Development* (Dar-es-Salaam: Oxford University Press 1973).
Nzula, A. J., *Forced Labour in Colonial Africa* (Zed Press 1979).

Oxaal, I., Barnett, T. and Booth, D., *Beyond the Sociology of Development* (Routledge and Kegan Paul 1975).

Parkin, D. J., *Palms, Wine and Witnesses* (Intertext Books 1972).

Parsons, T., *The Evolution of Societies*, edited and with an introduction by Toby, J. (Englewood Cliffs: Prentice Hall 1977).

Patterson, S., *Dark Strangers* (Tavistock 1963).

Peace, A., *Choice, Class and Conflict* (Harvester Press 1979).

Pons, V., *Stanleyville* (Oxford University Press 1969).

Poulantzas, N., *Political Power and Social Classes* (New Left Books 1973).

Redfield, R., *The Primitive World and its Transformations* (New York: Cornell University Press 1953).

Richards, E., *A History of the Highland Clearances* (Croom Helm 1983).

Rogers, B., *The Domestication of Women* (Kogan Page 1980).

Rose, G., *Deciphering Sociological Research* (Macmillan 1979).

Rose, S., Kamin, L. and Lewontin, R., *Not in Our Genes* (Penguin Books 1984).

Rostow, W. W., *The Stages of Economic Growth: a non-communist manifesto* (Cambridge University Press 1960).

Safa, H. I. (ed.), *Towards a Political Economy of Urbanisation in Third World Countries* (New Delhi: Oxford University Press 1982).

Sahlins, M., *Stone Age Economics* (Tavistock 1974).

Sen, A. K., *Poverty and Famines* (Clarendon Press 1984).

Shanin, T. and Alavi, H. (eds.), *Introduction to the Sociology of Developing Societies* (Macmillan 1982).

Skillen, R., *Ruling Illusions: Philosophy and Social Order* (Harvester Press 1977).

Smith, A., *The Wealth of Nations* (Penguin Books 1973).

Spencer, H., *The Evolution of Society* (Chicago: University of Chicago Press 1967).

Spender, D., *Man Made Language* (Routledge and Kegan Paul 1980).

Streeten P. and Jolly, R. (eds.), *Recent Issues in World Development* (Pergamon 1981).

Thomas, A. and Bernstein, H., *The Third World and Development* (Open University Press 1983).

Thompson, E. P., *The Making of the English Working Class* (Penguin 1978).

Wallerstein, I., *The Modern World System* (New York: Academic Press 1974).

Warren, B., *Imperialism: Pioneer of Capitalism* (Verso Books 1980).

Weber, M., *The Protestant Ethic and the Spirit of Capitalism* (Unwin 1967).

Wolf, E., *Peasant Wars of the Twentieth Century* (Faber 1971).

Worsley, P. M., *The Three Worlds* (Weidenfield and Nicholson 1986).

Young, K., Wolkowitz, R. and McCullagh, R., *Of Marriage and the Market* (CSE Books 1981).

Index

agrarian, and rural change 95
agribusiness 66, 122, 127–8
agricultural revolution 7
alienation 67, 219
Amin, S. 45, 187
anomie 67, 80, 219
Arusha Declaration 135
Articulation of modes of production 112, 220
Argentina, role of manufacturing in 43
Ashanti people of Ghana 98
assimilation of labour migrants 55, 60–1

Bangladesh, effects of Green Revolution 125
Bellah, R. 84
Bemba people of Zambia 57, 113
Black, C. E. 80
Blau, P. 108
'brain drain' 213–14; of doctors 214
Braudel, F. 14–15
Brazil, role of manufacturing in 43

Calvin, J. 28
capitalism: defined 27; growth of 6
capitalist: development 42–4; production and peasants 46
'capitalist underdevelopment' 40–1
Castells, E. 65; theory of urbanisation 65–6
Chayanov, A. V. 48, 116; theory of peasant household 116–17
Chile, underdevelopment of 41
Chodak, S. 25, 183–4
class: conflict 37; consciousness 71–2; and culture 58, 68–9, identity in Britain 58; and patriarchy 149–50; and peasantisation 114; role in social change 44–5; in rural society 112; struggle 37; in Third World cities 68–72; and tribe 57–8; *see also* social differentiation and gender
Club of Rome 189
Cohen, R. 188
'Cold War' and development of sociological theory 36–7
Colombian peasants 46–7
colonial state 131
colonialism and forced labour 98–9
colonisation, reasons for 97–9

Comte, A. 15–18, 31; and evolutionary development of society 15–16; and the reorganisation of society 16
Confucianism, and position of women 168
'contradiction', Marxist concept of 78–9
'convergence theory' of industrialisation 85–6
'culture of poverty' 60–1
Croll, E. 212

Das Kapital 79
Darwin, C. 200
Darwinism 200–1
decolonisation, and the development of sociological theory 36–7
decomposition of capital 92
dependency theory 42, 46; critique of 42–4; and education 138; and industrialisation 90
'deschooling' 145–6
development: defined 8–9; problems of defining 173–91
Djilas, M. 134
differentiation 220; *see also* social differentiation
'diploma disease' 142–3
Dore, R. 138, 142, 144
'dualism' 56
Durkheim, E. 4–5, 17, 31, 37, 54, 73, 93, 101, 103, 107, 108, 186; and class interests 138; and industrialisation 79; and science 25; and social solidarity 21–2, 31; theoretical language of 22; and urbanisation 55

education 137–47; 'deschooling' 145–6; 'diploma disease' 142–3; and economic growth 138–9, 141; and empowerment 144–7; and freedom 144–7; and industrialisation 140; Nyerere's views on 141; and the state 138, 142–4
Egypt, role of manufacturing in 43
Eisenstadt, S. 25, 73, 186
Engels, F. 36, 66, 158; *The Condition of the Working Class in England* 63